Praise for
*More Than a Match*

"Michael and Amy Smalley are among America's best at sharing God's truths in a profound yet entertaining and refreshing way. Like the couple who wrote it, this book will be a treasure you'll cherish!"

—DR. JOE WHITE, president of Kanakuk Kamps

"You won't meet a more authentic couple than Michael and Amy Smalley. There is help and encouragement on every page."

—JIM BURNS PHD, president of HomeWord and author of
*Creating an Intimate Marriage*

"I love Michael and Amy Smalley! Their wisdom and energy are only matched by their grounding in the sound principles of what truly makes couples work. For anyone searching for the secret to lasting love, I highly recommend you heed their advice."

—DR. KEVIN LEMAN, author of *Sheet Music: Uncovering the Secrets of Sexual Intimacy in Marriage*

More Than a Match

# More Than a Match

## How to Turn the Dating Game into Lasting Love

## Michael and Amy Smalley

### with Mike Yorkey

**WATERBROOK**
PRESS

MORE THAN A MATCH
PUBLISHED BY WATERBROOK PRESS
12265 Oracle Boulevard, Suite 200
Colorado Springs, Colorado 80921
*A division of Random House Inc.*

ISBN 978-1-4000-7304-7

Library of Congress Cataloging-in-Publication Data
Smalley, Michael.
    More than a match : how to turn the dating game into lasting love / Michael and Amy Smalley, with Mike Yorkey. — 1st ed.

    p. cm.

    ISBN-13: 978-1-4000-7304-7

    1. Mate selection—Religious aspects—Christianity. 2. Marriage—Religious aspects—Christianity. 3. Dating (Social customs)—Religious aspects—Christianity. I. Smalley, Amy. II. Yorkey, Mike. III. Title.

    BV835.S557 2006

    646.7'7—dc22

                              2006024012

Printed in the United States of America
2007—First Edition

10  9  8  7  6  5  4  3  2  1

# Contents

# Foreword

If you're familiar with my books, you may know that Michael will always be a living memorial of God's mercy to me. What you may not know is that Michael donated one of his kidneys to me in 2003. To see him now coming into his own, with his beautiful bride Amy by his side, fills me with a fatherly pride I can't deny.

As I said in *Making Love Last Forever,* the first step toward achieving the satisfaction of a lifelong love with your spouse is learning to love life itself—every part of it. My son Michael has always had that in abundance. So when I heard he and Amy were writing this book, *More Than a Match,* sharing the story of their love for life and each other, I was thrilled. This new book is nothing short of a full marriage course on how to win, keep, and sustain the lasting love every starry-eyed bride and groom dreams about.

If you want to find that perfect someone, get on a better path, or learn the secret to building a marriage that can stand the test of time, Michael and Amy's ideas and advice will help you get there.

I can think of no greater message for young people looking toward marriage today than the one put forward in this book. Read it, live it, and find yourself the deep satisfaction that comes in discovering *More Than a Match.*

—Gary Smalley

# Note to the Reader

In *More Than a Match,* we tell several stories about Amy Smalley's relationship with Jeff Miller (not his real name), to whom she was engaged to be married before that relationship ended.

As painful as the episode was for the both of them, Jeff has agreed to let us talk about that time in the hope that it will help you avoid the pain of a broken engagement. We thank Jeff for his courage and willingness to help others.

Elsewhere in this book, we have used pseudonyms for people we have met in our counseling sessions.

More Than a Match

# A Match Is Just a Click Away

**M**ichael: Falling in love for all the right reasons was turning out to be a real chore. Straightening up in my chair, I ran a hand through a thatch of hair and contemplated the bluish glow emanating from my PowerBook. The eight-hundred-pound gorilla in the cyber world of online dating, eHarmony.com, couldn't wait to match me with the woman of my dreams, but getting to the altar was taking some time. No sooner would I finish clicking my responses to one set of questions when another fresh set would leap before me.

"Please use the scale below to rate how well you believe each of the following words generally describes you," the screen directed.

In the left-hand column, fifteen adjectives were listed, including these four:

- content
- humorous
- efficient
- perfectionist

All I had to do was click a number on a scale of 1 to 7 with 1 being "not at all" and 7 meaning "very much so."

Let's see…content…I'm pretty contented these days. That's a 6. Humorous? People do say I'm funny. I'm going to give myself a 7. Efficient. Can't say I'm a world-record holder in that department…better give myself a 2. Am I a perfectionist? That's an easy call—not in the least. I'll take a 1.

And so it went. But after a half hour of point and click, I was only one-third of the way through eHarmony.com's self-personality test. The electronic information gathering was getting more interesting, though. On one screen page, I was asked to rate myself on another 1 to 7 scale regarding the following statements:

- "I enjoy mingling with people on social occasions."
- "I like reading everything I can about a subject."
- "I have a high desire for sexual activity."

*Oh yeah, I'm a 7 on all of those!*

Ninety minutes later, I finished answering the last of 436 questions. I sent my completed eHarmony.com profile into cyberspace, where a massive server churned my reams of personal information for several nanoseconds, seeking to match me in twenty-nine areas of compatibility with the millions of eHarmony.com ladies in its database.

Several minutes later, some very good news was waiting for me in my in box. I had some matches! An eHarmony.com e-mail informed me that five totally foxy women were waiting to hear from me, but before I could see what they looked like or read their profiles, a little business had to be contracted: a payment of $49.95, which would give me access to eHarmony's little black book for the next month.

At that point, my research was over, since I'm a married man. In addition, the knowledge that my wife, Amy, would do a "John Bobbitt" on me for following through on that step was more than enough incentive to let things go with eHarmony.com.

**Amy:** If you don't know who John Bobbitt is, just Google his name. I'm glad Michael wandered through the garden of online dating, though, which these days is more like the size of Central Park than a backyard plot. According to the research firm Pew Internet, 11 percent of all American, Internet-using adults—about sixteen million people—say they have gone to a dating Web site or another site where they can meet people online, making online dating one of the most lucrative Web businesses out there.[1] (Unfortunately, porn is probably number one, but those revenue figures are hard to track.)

In addition, men and women are meeting each other through community Web sites like MySpace.com, Friendster.com, Facebook.com, and Bebo.com, which are free services that use the Internet for communication through an interactive network of photos, chat rooms, Weblogs, and user profiles.

The more serious-minded gravitate toward online dating sites to find a perfect match rather than just a date, and some serious matching has gone on: Pew Internet said that 26 percent of American adults—fifty-three million people—have gone on a date with a person they met through a dating site.[2] About two million Americans have met their spouses through online dating, according to a *Wall Street Journal* article.[3]

The explosive rise in online dating has sparked some interesting ancillary Web sites. VerifiedPerson.com tracks age, residence, criminal record, and marital status of people you're interested in. DontDateHimGirl.com provides women with a forum—including a place to post pictures and an easy-to-use, searchable database—to share their experiences with men who have allegedly cheated. And LookBetterOnline.com lets you put your best foot—uh, face—forward by linking you with a local photographer who can provide professional, date-stamped portraits for your dating profile.

Looking your best for Mr. Right or Ms. Right has swelled to a five-hundred-million dollar industry,[4] with most of the action happening at online dating companies like eHarmony.com and Match.com as well as hundreds of rudimentary "post-a-picture" sites. Once seen as the refuge of the semi-desperate, online dating is more than a trend—it's here to stay. Singles have discovered a brave new world where boy-meets-girl is no longer limited by the boundaries of geography. In cyberspace, a match is just a click away.

## Down-Home Demeanor

**Michael:** The online dating site that intrigues me the most is eHarmony .com, founded by Neil Clark Warren, who has a doctorate in psychology and was once dean of Fuller Theological Seminary's graduate school of psychology. Anyone who watches cable TV is sure to have seen one of his folksy pitches for eHarmony.com.

I smile each time I see one of those brightly lit commercials because I knew Neil Clark Warren before he was known as Neil Clark Warren. Back in the 1980s and early 1990s, Dr. Warren wrote several books in the same vein as my father, Gary Smalley—self-help titles like *Finding the Love of Your Life* and *Date...or Soul Mate? How to Know If Someone Is Worth Pursuing in Two Dates or Less*. Like my father, Dr. Warren was a frequent guest on the Focus on the Family radio broadcast, batting ideas back and forth with Dr. James Dobson on how listeners could find the right mates, improve their communication skills, and build marriages that last.

Then the World Wide Web brought the Internet to the masses in the latter half of the 1990s, and the entrepreneurial Dr. Warren and his investors (who included my father), jumped into the dotcom craze with an idea that actually worked. Since its debut in 2000, eHarmony.com has become such a financial and cultural success that Jay Leno parodied Neil Clark Warren by wearing a wig in a *Tonight Show* skit: "Turns out that Saddam Hussein is a neat freak who likes to eat Doritos and Cheetos all day," joked Leno. "At least, that's what he said on his profile for eHarmony.com."

The buzzword you hear about online dating these days is *compatibility*, which is promoted as the key to success in a long-term relationship. With a warm and encouraging demeanor, Dr. Warren reminds TV viewers that eHarmony.com creates compatible matches based on twenty-nine dimensions proven to predict happier, healthier relationships. The happiest couples, he says, tend to have similar levels of intelligence, energy, and ambition, and they clearly enjoy doing things together.

I nod my head in agreement, but only up to a point. Sure, compatibility is great. Who would want to spend the rest of his or her life with someone who doesn't share similar outlooks, desires, and tastes? Where Amy and I part ways with the online dating world is with the notion that all you need to succeed in love is to sprinkle the pixie dust of compatibility on the relationship and you're a match.

Wrong! Compatibility is *not* the most important element to a successful relationship. Every person should enter a dating relationship with as much knowledge and skill as possible, and then continue on the same path of gaining more wisdom and understanding. Unfortunately, some people scroll through a list of matches and create images in their minds, and rarely do those images match up with reality.

**Amy:** What these online dating services overlook is that finding a compatible person is far easier than mastering what it takes to make a relationship work long term. Compatibility is the easy part; learning how to love is the more difficult task. Compatibility doesn't mean happiness.

What are some things that couples need to master before they are truly compatible? I believe couples on the road to marriage must learn how to communicate, how to forgive, how to get rid of anger, how to create safety in their relationships, and how to resolve conflict. That's why Michael and I are writing *More Than a Match*. We want to teach couples how to arrive at win-win solutions for the issues threatening to divide them.

When you *really* like someone—someone you think you may marry—it's imperative that you ask the big questions. Many times couples in a relationship assume they know all the big questions to ask. Our encouragement to you is, don't let any of these questions fall through the cracks. A third party can help guide your discussion, possibly seeing areas of weakness you might miss. Michael and I know that *More Than a Match* cannot be that third party, but we can guarantee that you will be *far* better prepared to answer many of the biggies if you stay with us throughout the pages of this book.

We want to spare you the nightmare that was our first year of marriage. Michael and I got married without the benefit of premarital counseling—*in-depth* premarital counseling. We met with a well-meaning pastor a couple of times, but we only skimmed some of the hot-button issues, much like a flat rock that skips across a glassy lake surface. In our naiveté, we thought we didn't need to dive into a full discussion of typical premarital issues for two reasons:

1. We were madly in love, so much so that we sailed through our courtship days with nary an argument in sight.
2. Michael was the son of a famous marriage expert, so he had soaked up all his father's wisdom and experience, right?

How wrong we were, as you'll soon discover.

## THE HONEYMOONERS

**Michael:** It all happened on the first day of the rest of our lives together—day one of our honeymoon.

Let me set the stage for you. Just twenty-four hours earlier, "I, Michael Thomas Smalley," had taken "Amy Renée Johnston to be my lawfully wedded wife, to have and to hold from this day forward, for better or worse, for richer or poorer, in sickness and in health, to love and to cherish until death do us part." I'm sure more than a few of the several hundred friends and family in attendance dabbed their eyes as they witnessed such a lovely wedding ceremony, complete with the symbolic and solemn lighting of white candles.

My father, Gary Smalley, married us. Not many people know that Dad is an ordained minister. We eagerly asked him to officiate the wedding, which was held at the charming and traditional Seventh and James Baptist Church across the street from the Baylor University campus in Waco, Texas.

*Officiate* is a funny word. No, Dad didn't wear a referee's black-and-white shirt, although he nearly blew a call when, at the end of the wedding, he kept coming up with announcement after announcement, like where the reception was being held and directions to get there. Meanwhile Amy and I were obviously waiting for him to say, "And now, you may kiss the bride." The audience tittered as I rocked on my heels awaiting the go signal from Dad. I really think he was embarrassed that his son was going to kiss in public!

The rest of our wedding day was a blur—except for that magical moment when Amy and I consummated our relationship for the first time in the honeymoon suite of the Marriott Hotel near the Dallas/Fort Worth International Airport (DFW). I'll have more to say about that rockets'-red-glare moment later on, but let me tell you, I was on a high after that…and after that…and after that. I don't think the two of us slept a wink before our early morning wake-up call to catch our flight from DFW to San Juan, Puerto Rico—the official start of our seven-day honeymoon trip, high-lighted by a cruise aboard the Norwegian Cruise Line's ship *Windward.*

Amy had asked me to plan the honeymoon, but we both agreed that we would not travel to any romantic places where she had spent time with her former fiancé, Jeff, and his family. I may be stupid, but I wasn't dumb: the idea of walking hand in hand with Amy along the *same* moonlit beach that she and Jeff had strolled didn't sit well with me. For the longest time I couldn't even say Jeff's name; I referred to him as "him."

Thinking that I had that bit of business taken care of, I had a great time flipping through glossy travel brochures showing heart-shaped hot tubs in hotel rooms and couples in postcoital glow, basking in the warmth of doing what honeymooning couples do. When I asked Amy what she thought about taking a Caribbean cruise, she squealed in delight. Since we were getting married in early December, the chance to warm ourselves on the sun-drenched decks of a cruise ship plying the Caribbean sounded wonderful.

As our plane made its final descent into San Juan's Luis Muñoz Marin International Airport, I happened to be thumbing through a San Juan guidebook. The plan called for us to spend the day and evening in San Juan before boarding the *Windward* the following morning.

I came across a stunning photo spread of Fort San Cristóbal, one of the largest defenses ever built in the Americas. The walls, with tunnels and bunkers, rose more than one hundred feet above sea level. Fort San Cristóbal was a short taxi ride from San Juan.

"Ooh, Amy, look at this fort," I commented. "We should go see this place."

Amy strained for a closer look. "Oh, yeah, we should. That was really fun."

Were my ears playing tricks on me? Past tense? "So, what do you mean, 'That *was* really fun'?"

Amy's eyes became really big. "Ah, nothing," she said, as she returned her gaze to the Puerto Rican countryside below us. "I don't mean anything by that."

"No, no. *Was* implies that you've been there before. Have you been to Fort San Cristóbal before?"

"No."

"What are you talking about? That doesn't make any sense. How would you know this fort would be fun?"

"Okay, I have been here."

"Oh. Who did you go with?"

"Nobody." The way she answered me so quickly told me she was lying through her pretty teeth.

"Nobody? Are you trying to tell me that you came all the way here to San Juan by yourself?"

"No, I...I came with *him* on a vacation trip with his mom and dad."

*Him? You mean Jeff, your old boyfriend?* I recoiled in horror—and immediately withdrew emotionally.

I had learned that tactic from my father, by the way. When he would get offended or hurt, he'd stop talking to Mom, my older sister and brother, and me. One time, we were taking a vacation in an RV—the kind with a little curtain between the driver and the back. We all knew Dad was ticked when he would pull that curtain and button it. He could go for *hours* without saying a word to anybody. We would try to break the logjam. We'd say, "Daaaad...," but he wouldn't budge. So, of course, that was my model for handling conflict.

I clammed up immediately with Amy. She tried to soothe my hurt feelings and do all the right things she'd read in my dad's books, such as being soft and issuing a heartfelt apology.

But I was wounded. I was mad.

I was also immature. I wouldn't talk to her. And I wouldn't let her touch me.

So we walked off the plane, ready to kick off our honeymoon, and we were not speaking to each other. We had been married less than twenty-four hours, including one sleepless, never-to-be-forgotten night. At the baggage claim area, I was *still* not talking to her.

"Where do we get our luggage?" she asked.

I refused to answer her. I just kept walking, and she followed. I was doing the full-on pout. It was pathetic.

As bags started to come out on the carousel, Amy asked, "Do you just want me to get the luggage? Or do you want to help?" We had checked four bags full of everything she *might* want to wear, including an oversized duffel bag full of her shoes.

Again, I didn't answer her. I kept shunning her. My big idea was that I would punish her by making her get all the luggage. That was real mature thinking. *I'll show her, ha, ha, ha.*

Out of the corner of my eye, I saw a blond, curly-headed gal come running toward me. *This is bizarre,* I thought. Before I could do anything, the young woman leaped at me, wrapped her arms around my neck, and screamed and hugged me in delight. I had absolutely no idea who she was.

Amy looked as flabbergasted as I had ever seen her. "Excuse me," she said, "but can you tell me what this is all about?"

Before I could answer my bride, I turned to the young woman who had given me a World Wrestling Entertainment bear hug. It turns out that I *did* remember who she was. Her name was Amy too!

"Amy, how nice to see you," I said, as I stepped back and took a look at the young woman. Yes, it was Amy from my high school days back in Scottsdale, Arizona—the girl who had broken my heart when she dumped me. *Oh yeah.*

"Michael, what are you doing here?" she giggled.

"I just got married, and we're here on our honeymoon. Amy, this is my wife, Amy."

"No! You're joking!" exclaimed my old girlfriend. "I just got married, and I'm here on *my* honeymoon too."

"When did you get married?"

"Yesterday."

"Well, so did we!" I said, as I turned to my Amy, who beamed the most plastic smile.

"Let me introduce you to my husband," the other Amy said, and hellos were made all around.

"What are you doing in San Juan?" I asked, immediately regretting asking such a stupid question, because I kind of knew what was coming.

"Oh, we're not going to be in San Juan very long," the old girlfriend said. "We board a cruise ship tomorrow for a week-long trip."

"What cruise ship are you going on?"

"The *Windward.*"

"The *Windward?* That's our cruise ship! Did you hear that, Amy?" I asked, as I turned my attention back to my bride. "Amy and Kevin are going to be on the same cruise as us!"

"How wonderful," said Amy, as plastic smile number two arrived on cue. "Small world. Wouldn't you say, honey?"

That's how our honeymoon started, and our barely-wet marriage began taking on more water from the minute we boarded the *Windward.* For the next several days, Amy and I fought like alley cats, scratching and clawing at each other, although we would kiss and make up so that we could make love before going at each other's throats again. Neither of us wanted to miss out on *that* part of the honeymoon.

And now this girl from high school who had tossed me overboard because she got the hots for the second-string quarterback—he wasn't even the starter!—was booked on the same Caribbean cruise with me. Our honeymoon became such a disaster that we left the *Windward* a day early and took a flight home from a Caribbean airport whose name escapes us to this day.

It would take nearly a year before our marriage entered safe harbor.

## Finding That Special Person

**Amy:** What an awful honeymoon! Looking back at that event, which happened a little more than a decade ago, still causes Michael and me to wince, but we're willing to get real—to use Dr. Phil McGraw's vernacular—to help you avoid some of the mistakes we made on the way to the altar and afterwards. To say that we've come a long way would be like Columbus informing Queen Isabella that his ship had crossed a lot of ocean to reach the New World.

Besides telling stories about ourselves in *More Than a Match,* we'll be sharing advice on finding the love of your life, based on our counseling experiences. Michael and I both have marriage and family counseling degrees and have worked with many premarital couples. Also, these days we travel through the United States and speak at weekend conferences about the skills needed to connect, love, and serve each other more effectively.

We love helping people learn what to look for in marriage partners and develop important love skills to ensure thriving and passionate marriages. *More Than a Match* will help you:

- prepare a list of qualities you would like to see in your potential mate
- know what a good dating life looks like
- create sexual boundaries

- end a relationship when it's not right
- resolve conflict
- accept personal responsibility in the relationship

As we considered putting our thoughts in print, we wanted to make sure that by the time you finish this book, you'll say, "Wow! Finding the love of my life is a lot more than just finding someone who's compatible with me. Now I know what it's going to take to stay committed for the long haul!" This will be the golden thread woven throughout *More Than a Match*.

It's been said that you should go into a relationship with your eyes wide open and then keep them shut after saying, "I do." But many couples do just the opposite: their eyes are blinded by love and swirling hormones and the notion that "this is it!" Unfortunately, it's only after the nuptials that there's a rude awakening: "Oh my goodness. What have I just done?"

In working with couples, Michael and I have found ourselves acting like doctors asked to treat the symptoms of disease. But, just as many medical practitioners preach preventive medicine, encouraging patients to take proactive steps to protect their health before disease strikes, we want to vaccinate you against the nasty divorce virus before your wedding day.

It seems that the counseling community has largely ignored this strategy. PREPARE/ENRICH founder Dr. David Olson estimates that only 10–15 percent of couples seek out extensive premarital counseling after they get engaged.[5] So look at *More Than a Match* as an inoculation against meeting the wrong person or starting your marriage off on the wrong foot, no matter how compatible an online dating site says you two are.

Whether you're in the midst of a successful online dating relationship, have recently met your honey at a church social, or are still in the looking stage, *More Than a Match* will help you see that real love is possible for you.

## Think About It

## Talk About It

- What are the positive things about online dating? the negative things about online dating?
- Why is "compatibility," as online dating sites define it, not a guarantee that a relationship will last long term?
- What do you think are the really big questions that need answers in a serious relationship?
- What do you think makes the difference in the great marriages you know of?

# Can You **Fall in Love** *and* **Be Compatible?**

**M**ichael: When I filled out my eHarmony.com questionnaire, it didn't take long to figure out that its massive mainframe computer was prompting me for my thoughts on what I liked to do, and didn't care to do, during my free time.

For instance, when it came to movies, I saw questions along these lines:

- Do you like scary movies or romantic movies?
- Do you like going out to see a first-run movie in the theaters, or do your prefer to rent a DVD and watch it at home?
- Do you even *like* movies?

When eHarmony.com and other online dating services ask questions like these, they are searching for ways to quantify compatibility in certain areas and incompatibility in others. They take your information and dump it into various buckets labeled with tags such as leisure activities, spiritual beliefs, and views on raising children, where it's churned and used to form your profile.

I see nothing wrong with using technology to pair unfamiliar people for a potentially long-term, romantic relationship. Online dating can work; Amy and I have counseled dozens of successful couples who first made a connection in cyberspace before getting to know each other. We also have spoken with a similar number of couples who have experienced rough patches in their relationships, many of them perplexed that they were having problems after a computer had declared them so compatible. What Amy and I think is that millions of singles have been conditioned by the warm, fuzzy ads for eHarmony.com, Match.com, and other online services to believe that compatibility is the most important element to a successful relationship.

Not so. In our view, compatibility can be the fool's gold in the world of boy-meets-girl. Sure, great relationships begin with like-minded individuals, but do couples really understand what it takes to live a lifetime in love and harmony? Not if they stop with compatibility! Thus, we see *More Than a Match* having a two-pronged purpose: pointing you toward the right partner and then teaching you the most important love skills to ensure a thriving and passionate relationship.

Once while on a plane ride from New York to Houston, I was outlining several chapter ideas for this book. I was seated next to an attractive woman named Gwyneth, who noticed the working title, *More Than a Match,* in big bold letters on my computer screen.

"Excuse me," she said with apprehension, "are you some kind of author?"

"Yes, I am," I said brightly.

"Sorry, but what's the book about?"

I smiled because I thought this would be a good opportunity to test my book idea on her. "It's called *More Than a Match,* and it's about how men and women can master and understand what makes a relationship successful in today's online dating world."

That was the only cue she needed. Suddenly, like the water that might have gushed through Hans Brinker's dike, her story rushed out like a rampaging flood. Gwyneth told me that her troubles began when she posted her photo and profile at a popular matchmaking site. After meeting the "perfect man" online, she quickly agreed to go out for dinner. From the moment she and her handsome date were seated, she found it easy to converse with him; after all, they had "a lot in common." They even joked about it.

Maybe it was the romantic atmosphere, or the third glass of wine, but when her date asked if she was up to "taking this party elsewhere," she knew what he meant. After all, this young woman, who looked to be in her late twenties, was a sophisticated Manhattan career woman who had been around the block a few times. Within the hour, they were hooking up back at her place. Gwyneth didn't see anything terribly wrong with this—I got the feeling that wasn't her first one-night stand—but her story turned to anguish when her new "boyfriend" suddenly stopped communicating.

In fact, she never heard from him again. "I felt used and abused," she said, tears welling up in her eyes. Gwyneth chalked up her experience to being taken advantage of by a sexual predator, someone who had used a matchmaking site to hook up with vulnerable singles such as herself.

"I'm sorry to hear about this," I said, shaking my head. "Your story is a reminder that I'm writing this book for people like you."

Amy: Gwyneth made a crucial but common mistake—believing that since she and her boy toy had similar interests, they were a match. The problem is that she blithely entered the relationship without knowing the purpose of dating, how to determine whether their personalities meshed, or how to ask the right questions regarding the future of the relationship, and without being aware of the importance of premarital counseling if the relationship advanced further down the road.

These strategies are part of *More Than a Match,* so that the next time you make a match in the online dating world—or meet someone the old-school way—you'll understand what it takes to love fully and what the fundamental truths of a successful marriage are. Because marriage—a long-lasting, happy one—should be your goal. It was certainly mine once I reached my twenties, but for Michael, he had been ready to get married for a long, long time.

## GETTING STARTED

Michael: "What do you want to be when you grow up?"

I was used to hearing that question, but that's because I was still a third grader. That question was huge on the playgrounds, and my buddies and I were always talking about what we wanted to be when we got older. Many of my friends said they wanted to become astronauts or firemen.

Not me.

"I want to be married," I announced for all to hear. The thought of growing up big and strong and becoming a husband and a dad appealed to me. I felt there was something magical about coming home to a nice house with a white picket fence and the smell of baked chicken cooking in the oven. Kissing my wife didn't sound like fun since she had cooties, but playing catch with my kids sure sounded great.

Why did I feel this way at such a young age? Looking back, I believe I thought marriage was cool and something to look forward to because I had a father who wrote books about being married and traveled to interesting places speaking about the topic.

Marriage is a many-splendored thing, and even though its popularity has waned in recent years, 95 percent of the U.S. population will give marriage a try at least once during their lifetimes, according to the U.S. Census Bureau.[1] Marriage has been around since Adam and Eve got hitched in the garden. You may not know this story, but back in the days when he was all alone, Adam was walking around one afternoon, feeling lonely. From His perch in heaven, God took notice and felt sorry for Adam. "Is there anything I can do for you?" God asked.

"Well, it would be nice to have someone to talk to," said Adam. "You seem awfully busy these days."

"Okay, tell you what. I'll create a companion for you. She'll be a woman. She'll gather food for you, cook for you, and when you discover clothing, she'll wash it for you. She'll agree with every decision you make. She'll bear your children and never ask you to get up in the middle of the night to care for them. She won't nag you, and she will always be the first to admit she was wrong when you disagree. She'll give you love and passion any time you want it, and she'll never go to bed with a headache."

"Wow, that sounds great!" said Adam, his interest rising. "What will a woman like this cost me?"

"An arm and a leg."

This seemed like a lot to Adam. Then he had a brainstorm. "What can I get for a rib?" he asked.

**Amy:** Typical Michael, working in a joke at poor Adam's expense. Down through the centuries, the institution of marriage (which is why some people joke that you need to be in an institution to want to be married) has been a constant in societies. From the broad plains of Kilimanjaro to the dense tropics of Malaysia to the fertile valleys of Israel, marriage has long been regarded as the foundation of a stable society. When a man and woman marry with the intention of staying together for life, it compels both parties to love, cherish, and work together for the long haul. The offspring of their union—children—blossom and grow when a father and mother are committed to each other and to the successful raising of the next generation.

These days, however, marriage is battered around like a piñata at a Cinco de Mayo party. It's certainly not revered or held up as something special, as it once was. High school reunion announcements invite you to attend with your spouse or significant other. Airline companion fares weren't invented with married couples in mind. Hollywood celebrities parade across the pages of *People* and *Us Weekly* with their latest boy toys or honey pots. Angelina Jolie, Brad Pitt, Ben Affleck, Jennifer Lopez, and other Hollywood A-listers have lived with a succession of lovers over the years, flaunting their love-'em-and-leave-'em lifestyles in alluring picture spreads dripping with attitude. Actor Chad Michael Murray was linked to Paris Hilton, married his WB costar Sophia Bush (and divorced her after five months), and within seven months was engaged to marry show extra Kenzie Dalton, who was eighteen years old at the time.

You have to wonder how seriously celebrities take the whole marriage thing. When Pamela Anderson of *Baywatch* fame exchanged vows with Mötley Crüe drummer Tommy Lee, she wore a white thong bikini. The society pages noted that he was resplendent in his swim trunks. Instead of a wedding ring, Pamela tattooed her husband's name on her finger. Not to be outdone, Tommy Lee is rumored to have tattooed her name on his unmentionables. Their marriage lasted three years and resulted in two children—and a couple of tattoos that needed to be removed. *Ouch!*

The media doesn't like to dwell on marital train wrecks like the one I just described. Instead, they prefer pumping out the following message: *Marriage? That's for insecure yokels living in flyover country. Hey, if you want to be cool, just live with her (or him). You'll have a great time, but don't worry if the relationship doesn't work out. Stuff happens.*

Today's TV sitcoms are great windows into the world of marriage. Married couples—if you can find any on *Sex and the City, Friends,* or *Seinfeld* reruns—are usually portrayed as dweebs who aren't hip enough to swim in the lake of live-in couples. Soooo last century. When's the last time you saw marital commitment celebrated on an episode of *Desperate Housewives?* Well, you'd have to use the flicker and go to Nick at Nite, home to those classic black-and-white *I Love Lucy* or *Leave It to Beaver* episodes from the fifties. Instead of Ricky and Lucy and Ward and June, we get dysfunctional couples like Al and Peg Bundy from *Married...With Children.*

This cultural dog pile on marriage has contributed to the inevitability of two trends never before seen in our history:

1. The skyrocketing number of couples living together, or shacking up, as conservative talk-show host Dr. Laura Schlessinger would say.

2. The new trend toward "starter marriages," in which couples fall in love and marry but there's no long-term expectation from either party that the marriage will last.

Let's take a closer look at these two phenomena.

## LIVING TOGETHER MEANS NEVER HAVING TO SAY YOU'RE SORRY?

In Hollywood, it's so simple: you fall in love, you move in together. Happens all the time in the movies, usually in the first reel. Living together is widely accepted, part of the cultural wallpaper, and not a big deal. You won't have Dear Abby breathing down your neck about immoral behavior if you ask her how to get your boyfriend to pick up his dirty socks. But you may end up seeking a roommate in the want-ad section of the Sunday newspaper because your girlfriend moved out for another guy and you need help paying the rent.

To show how commonplace living together has become, back in 1960 there was one cohabiting couple for every ninety married couples; today, there is one cohabiting couple for every *twelve* married couples. More than half (56 percent) of all first marriages today are preceded by cohabitation, according to the National Marriage Project.[2]

We know from our counseling experience that living together isn't considered a big deal, because we've had plenty of young couples raised in *Christian* homes inform us that they're sharing the same roof without the benefit of matrimony. Many tell us they were conned by their parents to see us. The pretense? To make sure they were the right match for each other—in other words, compatible.

We love it when live-in couples come see us for counseling. Not because we want to tell them they're going straight to hell (which wouldn't do any good anyway), but because we relish engaging them in a discussion about cohabitation. We also understand what our generation is thinking. It's not that Gen Xers are antimarriage, although cohabitation rates have soared in recent years; it's that Michael and I are antidivorce.

Let me explain further. Back in the 1960s and 1970s, when our parents were marrying, the smaller numbers of those cohabiting were antimarriage because it was popular to be antiestablishment. Today, many couples are living together because they want to spare themselves the pain of marital breakup; they have seen their parents divorce in record numbers. In other words, they are living together to see whether things work out before permanently tying the knot. Better a busted live-in arrangement than a busted marriage.

Here's what we say: if you want your relationship to last—and what dreamy-eyed couple wouldn't want their relationship to last a long, long time—then the worst thing you can do is to live together before you're married. The cold, hard facts of social research—secular, Christian, whatever—have all found that couples who live together before marriage have significantly higher divorce rates.

Depending on which study you refer to, the risk of divorce after living together can be 40–85 percent higher than the risk of divorce after not living together. Phrased another way, couples who live together before marriage are almost twice as likely to divorce when compared to those who do not live together. Nobody must be listening to this message, because social science researchers are predicting that there will be just seven married couples for every cohabiting couple by 2010. That's just around the corner, friend.

**Michael:** So, whether you are living together or thinking about shacking up with your honey, let us offer these arguments against the practice.

**You're going to have better sex if you don't live together.** Yes, you heard us right, and we're leading with this argument because many guys view living together as a casual arrangement that guarantees lots of sex and a way to get out of cooking and doing the laundry. You know the old saying: why pay for the cow when the milk is free? Studies have shown, however, that sexual satisfaction rises considerably after marriage, especially if you haven't jumped the gun. Researchers at State University of New York and the University of Chicago found that of all sexually active people, those who reported being most physically pleased and emotionally satisfied were married couples.

In chapter 7, we'll be getting into all the biblical reasons why it's better to wait, but God knew what He was doing when He reserved sexual relations for married couples—no disease, no heartbreak, and no comparisons to former lovers.

**You're going to live longer and live healthier.** Researchers learned that married people have longer life expectancies, experience better health, and contract less disease. And if you and your special one marry as virgins, you will not be bringing a sexually transmitted disease to the marriage bed. The Centers for Disease Control and Prevention estimates that nineteen million new infections occur each year, with almost half of them among young people ages fifteen to twenty-four. [3]

**You're going to be better off financially.** Don't two people live as cheaply as one? But what you save on buying a bigger box of Wheaties must be offset by the emotional and spiritual costs of cohabitation—and those are pretty high, based on the pain and sorrow that we have witnessed. And live-in split-ups can be just as messy as marital breakups: someone is usually left holding the credit card bills for all the furniture, kitchen items, and other stuff that couples tend to accumulate.

**You're unlikely to get beat up or abused.** According to the U.S. Department of Justice, nearly half of all family violence is committed by boyfriends, girlfriends, or ex-spouses, but only 25 percent can be attributed to spouses.[4] (And don't forget that there are twelve married couples for every cohabiting couple.[5]) Bottom line: boyfriends are more likely to beat you up, not husbands.

**You won't play second fiddle.** Rutgers University researchers working with the National Marriage Project released a report about why men are afraid to commit to marriage these days. The report listed the usual suspects: men can get all the sex they want without marrying, still hang out with their friends in sports bars, and avoid the financial pitfalls of divorce.[6] The most galling admission, says author and speaker Chuck Colson, is that men "don't want to marry their girlfriends because they're waiting for their 'true love' to come along. Then they'll tie the knot, buy a home, and father kids. Meanwhile, their live-ins can pick up their socks and provide sex on demand."[7] Did you catch that, ladies? He's living with you because he doesn't see you as marriage material. How does that make you feel?

**Your family won't have to reserve their affections.** The cultural voices claim that living together is a more enlightened way to find out if your relationship will last. They say that two people who love each other should be the only necessary ingredients for making a good partnership, that anyone who attempts to attach a social stigma to living together—like calling it living in sin—should be silenced because that shows intolerance to the way that some people want to live.

That's what we're told society thinks. But what about your parents? sisters and brothers? Wouldn't you be cheating them out of something by moving in with someone? They would have to hold back their love, keep their emotions in check, because they couldn't give themselves whole heartedly to someone who they know might not be around the next time the family gathers at Thanksgiving or Christmas. Besides, you know what they're thinking: *That living arrangement is not right in the eyes of God.*

**You won't have to make excuses later in life.** Dr. Laura Schlessinger took a great phone call on her radio program one day from a woman saying that her teenage sons wanted to quit playing football, but "their father" wanted them to keep playing the sport.

Dr. Laura's ears perked up. "Are you divorced?" she asked.

"No, I've been living with him for fourteen years."

"You what?" Dr. Laura exclaimed. After she calmed down, she asked the caller if her partner was there.

"Yes, he's here."

"Can you put him on the phone too?

When the man got on the phone, Dr. Laura asked him to tell her why he wanted his two sons to stay on the football team. When Dr. Laura asked him why this was so important to him, he said, "I want to teach them about commitment."

"Commitment?" the talk-show host countered. "You've been teaching them the meaning of commitment for fourteen years."

Play of the day.

## MOVING ON UP?

**Amy:** The second trend we are seeing is the rise in starter marriages, where the first marriage is viewed as a stepping stone to the next (hopefully better) marriage—much like how young families buy starter homes with expectations of moving up when promotions and salary raises happen at work.

The U.S. Census Bureau doesn't track starter marriages, but the term generally applies to childless couples in their twenties who stay married for fewer than five years before dissolving the unions. Since the marriage did not produce any children, both sides view the experience as a dress rehearsal, much the way that plays and musicals start off Broadway before heading for the Big Apple. "If people are going to divorce, better to do so after a brief marriage in which no children suffer the consequences," said Pamela Paul, author of a provocative book called *The Starter Marriage and the Future of Matrimony.*[8]

Pamela Paul, whose first marriage ended in divorce before the first anniversary, smelled a good book idea when she noticed that many of her twenty-something friends were marrying and quickly divorcing as well. After conducting more than sixty interviews with starter-marriage dropouts, she concluded that most young couples were marrying because they had finished school and needed someone to cling to or because they felt that a great marriage would jump-start a fabulous career. (Think power couples.)

Ms. Paul adds that many young couples focus on the wedding day and the fancy reception and the three-tiered wedding cake, but not the big picture, which is the lifelong commitment.[9] Then again, we are the children of the first generation to divorce in massive numbers. Chances are you have grown up in a home where:

- Dad and Mom never formalized their relationship.
- Dad and Mom divorced before you became an adult.
- Mom never married, so you were raised in a single-parent home.
- Mom or Dad remarried after the divorce, so you were raised with a biological parent and a stepparent.

Michael and I know how fortunate we are to have grown up in homes where our parents are still working on their marriages more than forty years after their wedding dances. You may not understand what you missed out on by not growing up in a two-parent home. It's too late to do anything about that, but it's not too late to choose the best approach possible to finding that special person God has waiting for you.

If you're between the ages of eighteen and thirty-five, you belong to the most highly prized demographic in our culture. You are the tail that wags the dog. Advertisers swoon over you, Hollywood targets more films and TV shows your way, and credit card companies fall over themselves trying to get your business. These are the high-spending years, the time you will finish your schooling, start a career, meet and date others of the opposite sex, fall in love, marry, and start a family. That's a blueprint of what should happen in this fabulous mystery called life. Although we sometimes take detours from this primrose path, it's best not to mix and match too much with the order we just described.

So, you're probably in the middle of the bull's-eye for this guy-girl thing, and some wonderful experiences and important decisions lie ahead. Because choosing *who* to marry will affect generations to come, it's best not to get ahead of God on this one. We think that before you do anything else, you should ask God to play the role of matchmaker, even if you're using the services of eHarmony.com or Match.com. We call it praying your way to a great mate.

**Michael:** While prayer is vital, there are some compatibility factors that you need to be aware of, factors that show what it *really* means to be compatible. Before we reveal those, though, we're going to tell how we met thirteen years ago—long before eHarmony.com was a glint in the eye of Neil Clark Warren. Our story is instructive because we are two people no computer would have matched, yet we found each other and fell in love.

**Think About It**

## Talk About It

- Why do you think so many couples live together before they marry?
- What are the compelling reasons *not* to live together before marriage?
- Can you sense God's peace in your life today?
- What are your personal reasons for your current living arrangement?

# Touched by **an Angel**

**M**ichael: In the spring of my freshman year at Baylor University, a couple of dorm buddies asked me to go watch the cheerleading tryouts being held at the intramural fields. People take their football pretty seriously in Texas, and where there's a football game being played, there's sure to be a bevy of beautiful female cheerleaders waving pompoms and buff male cheerleaders yelling into megaphones. The big thing at Baylor football games was the bear claw—the curving of all five fingers inward to form a bear claw—and the "Sic 'em, Bears" yell, which symbolized pride in Baylor athletics.

"You have *got* to go with us," said Brodie, while his sidekick, Troy, grinned like a junior-high kid attending his first dance. "There's this hot girl you've got to check out."

Brodie and Troy informed me that they had noticed her from their perch next to Burleson statue, where they watched the pretty girls stride by on their way to class. Since the idea of observing cheerleading tryouts sounded like a nice diversion, I made plans to join them.

On the afternoon of the yell-team tryouts, I was one of perhaps four hundred people sitting in a small grandstand, taking it all in.

"See her?" Brodie asked. "She's the one on the far left."

*Oh my goodness, what a babe,* I thought. *She's drop-dead gorgeous.* I didn't start drooling on myself, but my eyes locked in on the pixie-eyed, auburn-haired, five-foot, three-inch, one-hundred-pound, cutest little thing stretching her hamstrings on the grass.

The testosterone tachometer must have been climbing for Brodie and Troy as well, seated to the right and left of me. As if on cue, they stood up and obnoxiously yelled, "Amy!"

*So that's her name. Amy…what a beautiful name, like something out of a fairy tale.* I acted as though I'd never heard such an enchanting name before—I was so obviously caught up in my emotions and not wanting to believe that such a princess could have such a name.

Amy looked up toward the stands to see what the ruckus was about. When she glanced our way, I looked full into her face. I was instantly awestruck. Something deep in her brown eyes mesmerized me. Never before in my life had I looked into the eyes of such inner beauty. If someone could have looked inside my addled brain at that moment, he would have seen all sorts of colored lights blinking and blown fuses exploding, and heard loud horns blaring. Amy had definitely pushed my attraction buttons! I must have looked like Patrick from *SpongeBob Square Pants,* a bumbling, dumb-faced cartoon character.

My reverie was broken when the whistle blew, signaling the start of cheerleading tryouts. One by one, the energetic guys and girls tumbled and cheered for the crowd, because it was we who would cast our votes for our future cheerleaders. In the midst of all the excitement, I noticed Amy glancing my way. My thoughts ran wild. *Has she noticed me?*

**Amy:** I looked up and saw two guys drop to their knees and chant, "We're not worthy, we're not worthy!"—the famous tagline from the film *Wayne's World*. Everybody was looking and laughing at these two guys acting like dorks. I can remember looking up and smirking at two of Baylor's biggest knuckleheads, but they kept on chanting, "We're not worthy, we're not worthy," anyway. It was sweet but lame.

**Michael:** I remember things a bit differently. When Amy gazed up from the field, our eyes met, pressing my attraction buttons again. I panicked! This Amy was special, and I felt that destiny had finally knocked on my door.

Yep, I was whipped after that first gaze from afar. I returned to my dorm room, where I was inspired to write some puppy-love poetry that I'm embarrassed to share, but it reveals how love-struck I was that afternoon:

**A Love Story**
I saw you standing in all your glory,
Smiling, laughing, but not knowing me.
I gazed upon you with eyes of merry,
But still your eyes looked farther past me.
For you could not know the way I felt,
The words between us were few and far.
But deep within my heart of hearts,
I knew you'd see me, like the morning star.

I couldn't wait to meet her for the first time. Then one day while walking to class, I actually saw Amy running toward me. Confused and scared, I stood my ground and didn't move—hoping, praying that I was the one she was running to. As she approached, Amy walked right up to me and looked deeply in my eyes, but said nothing. Her eyes moistened for a moment before she tenderly reached out and touched my face with her soft hand. In a gentle voice, she cooed, "I love you."

Before I could reply, I painfully woke up from my dream.

## AMY'S WORLD

I had to meet this goddess, but I knew that hanging around Burleson statue and moaning, "We're not worthy," wasn't going to land me her phone number. I wanted to become part of Amy's world, not *Wayne's World*.

That thought bounced around my mind for several weeks until I spoke with a friend named Michael who told me that he was planning to try out for the basketball cheerleading team.

"You mean there are different cheerleaders for the football team and the basketball team?" I asked.

"Yep," said Michael. "What you voted for were the football cheerleaders. Everyone wants to be in Floyd Casey Stadium on Saturday afternoons and travel with the Bears football team to away games. There isn't that much interest in cheerleading at the basketball games, however. In fact, we need some extra guys. Would you be interested?"

"Nah, I don't think so." I didn't hold male cheerleaders in the highest regard and, while in high school, had thought of them as sissies. Didn't seem like a guy thing to me. The thought of dressing in snow-white seer-sucker pants and a white letter sweater while screaming, "Sic 'em, Bears," didn't sound like the way I wanted to spend my Saturdays. Growing up, I was used to *playing* sports (I was a four-sport athlete in high school, earning letters in football, basketball, tennis, and track), not *cheering* others from the sidelines.

"You should think about it," Michael insisted. "The basketball cheer-leading squad practices with the football squad."

*Wait a minute. Amy is on the football cheerleading team.* If I got picked as a basketball cheerleader, I could really get to know her.

"When did you say those basketball tryouts were?" I asked.

"Next fall, as soon as school starts."

I had a lot to learn about cheerleading. First of all, they didn't call them cheerleaders at Baylor, they were members of the yell squad. And male yell leaders didn't do a lot of yelling through megaphones. Instead, they performed stunts with a female partner, athletic moves like lifting the girl's body and flipping her in the air and catching her, resulting in much close, hand-to-body contact. But I wasn't thinking about touching Amy yet. (Hey, I was an honorable guy!) I just wanted to get to know her.

That summer, I worked at a sports camp as a counselor, but I spent every free moment teaching myself to tumble and perform standing back-flips. I ran through the forest to get in the best hard-body shape of my life. Think *Rocky* in a boater hat and letter sweater. *Getting stronger...*

In the fall, I showed up for the basketball yell-team tryouts totally petrified. I only knew the most basic stunts, so I was greatly worried that my inexperience would cost me my shot to make the team and meet Amy.

Five other guys and I were directed to sit down on the gym bleachers.

"Here's the deal, guys," said the yell-team coach. "No tryouts today. You all make the team." It turned out that the basketball yell team needed six guys, and since six had showed up for tryouts, we all were in.

As promised, the basketball yell team did practice with the football cheerleaders. I was careful not to come on too strong to Amy, which meant I was learning to patiently bide my time. She seemed like the real deal, and I didn't want to scare her away. I'll never forget the first time, though, that I died and went to heaven.

We were practicing partner stunts in the gym one afternoon, where the guys hold and lift the girls into the air and do tricks. Everyone had a partner except for me since I was so new to the yell squad.

Amy noticed that I didn't have anyone to practice with. She came over and asked, "Hey, do you know how to do an extension?"

I knew what an extension was. You lift the girl up to your chest, and then you raise her so that she can stand on your hands above your head. The only problem was that I had never done this rather advanced stunt before.

"Sure," I found myself saying. "Do you want to practice a few?" *Please say yes. Please say yes.*

"Okay," she said. Amy grabbed my hand—that first touch was special—and led me to the center of the gym. All my senses were on overdrive at that point—Amy and I had just had our first conversation and now we were holding hands! Who cares if I told a little fib?

Amy turned and faced me while putting her hands on her hips. That was my signal to go. I reached out and placed my hands around her tiny waist. She bobbed twice, and on the second hop, I lifted her into the air and bent back a little so that she could rest her feet on my chest. Once she did that, I started wobbling some.

"Are you okay?" she asked.

"I think so," I huffed and puffed. "Here goes."

I bench-pressed her tiny frame above my head with her feet capped in my two hands. My arms shook, not because she was heavy, but because I was new to this stunt. I'm sure my inexperience didn't engender the greatest amount of confidence in my newfound partner since she was depending on me not to drop her on the gym floor.

After holding her aloft for a few moments, I asked, "Cradle?" This was my signal, asking if she wanted to dismount. If she said yes, I would toss her in the air and catch her like a mom cradles a baby.

"No, I think I'll just come down," she said.

*Rats!*

## FAST FRIENDS

I was too timid to send out signals regarding my real feelings about Amy. It's not that I put her on this pedestal, but she was way too beautiful, way too captivating, way too enchanting, and way too together for a schlep like me. I was happy just to interact with her on the yell team, although I spent many nights dreaming of what it would be like to marry her.

The good news was that we were becoming fast friends. I walked her from yell practice back to her car, let her borrow my camera for a photography class (I had fun showing her how to use it), and sipped Cokes with her in the student union, where I confided my interest in other girls to Amy. I never confided my bubbling-beneath-the-surface interest in her, however.

Then came the Saturday morning of the big football game against one of our conference rivals, SMU, Southern Methodist University. We were starting to warm up at the stadium—I had been promoted to the football yell squad—when a squealing Amy ran up and jumped into my arms.

"Whoa, and to what do I owe this pleasure?" I asked.

"Here," she said, as she held out her left hand. There on her ring finger was the fattest diamond engagement ring I had ever seen—that rock must have been ten carats. Though she didn't know it, I felt a cold dagger stab into my heart. She had never told me about this boyfriend, and now they were to be married! *But Amy! What about you and me?*

"So, what do you think?" Amy asked, seeking my approval.

"The ring is beautiful," I managed. "I'm very happy for you." *And really bummed for myself.* "Who's the lucky guy?"

"Jeff, my boyfriend from the University of Texas."

## UNCERTAIN TIMES

Let's fast-forward to the following spring. In April 1994, Amy was feeling extremely uncomfortable at a time when her future should have never looked brighter. She would be graduating in June, and in December, she and her fiancé were planning on starting a new life together as Mr. and Mrs. Jeff Miller.

**Amy:** That spring, as I prepared to graduate, I had never been so diligent in prayer. Every day I wrote down my prayers in a prayer journal. For me, it was a talk-to-God quiet time. I would study the Bible, and then I would write in my journal. I was feeling, *I have to get some peace with this.*

The wedding plans? Well, we had gotten engaged the previous October, and now it was late April. We had a date set for December 3, a fourteen-month engagement. That's a long time to wait, and now Jeff was not sure that he was ready to commit to that date. We were fighting more and more. We had grown up in different denominations—he was Catholic and I was Southern Baptist. That meant that we were used to very different styles of worship and ways of relating to God.

**Michael:** I knew I had to let go of the special person I had secretly loved. When the opportunity came for me to shore up my Spanish requirements by going to Mazatlán, Mexico, as part of a Baylor study-abroad summer program, I thought the change of scenery would do me good. I made plans at the end of my junior year to fly to Mazatlán for the six-week intensive program.

Prior to my departure, my prayer time with God was as rich as it had ever been. The best part of Amy's engagement was that it brought me closer to God. When times get tough, I naturally get closer to Christ, and that was one of those occasions. I remember praying, "Lord, Amy has all the qualities I'm looking for, but if I can't have her, then I know the girl You have for me must be even better. I can't wait to meet her."

I knew God always worked both sides of the equation. If Amy was not the one for me, then God was orchestrating something else. I think I prayed every day to meet the woman who would take Amy's place, although I didn't think that was possible. Who could take the place of "my" Amy Renée Johnston?

Before I left for Mazatlán, my plans were to fly to New York City with my dad, where he planned to film an eighteen-part video series called *Hidden Keys to Loving Relationships* with Frank Gifford and his wife, Kathie Lee, of *Live with Regis and Kathie Lee* fame. The video series would go on to sell four million copies. I was invited to sit in at the filming, and Dad told me if I played my cards right, he'd find a cameo role for me.

I was driving along Interstate 35, leaving Waco for Branson before flying to New York. Now, I'm not being hokey about this, but I believe God prompted me to get off the interstate and drive by Amy's apartment to see her before I continued on through Dallas.

**Amy:** I hung up the phone in a jumble of tears—and then I heard the knock.

"Michael!" I fell into his arms and sobbed and sobbed. He was such a comfort. He was a friend. I knew how compassionate he was. I knew he would understand. I knew he would be there for me. I hugged him and started crying, and I held on tight for a long time.

"Amy, what's wrong?" he asked.

"It's Jeff," she sniffled. "He says he doesn't know why, but he's not going to be ready to get married in December. And when we do get married, he wants to get married in his church." I started wailing again.

The differences between Roman Catholics and Southern Baptists were starting to rear their heads. There were times when I went to his church and he went to mine, but when it came down to crunch time and we had to pick a church to get married in, we were at loggerheads. My parents were between churches, so Jeff said, "We can get married in my church."

But I didn't want to get married in a Catholic church, so how were we to "become one"? I knew I was supposed to be submissive, so I talked to a Catholic priest one on one, but I never got a real good answer to bridge that gulf. He was kind and compassionate, saying things like, "This is a big decision," but that wasn't a huge help.

The whole thing became so overwhelming. My plan was to get married on the first Saturday in December, so when Jeff told me he wasn't ready, that sent a strong signal that he was wavering. And *that* made me waver.

Just that morning, I had prayed for peace about my decision to marry Jeff. My world was in chaos. Then Michael stopped by.

**Michael:** I felt very calm as I consoled Amy. *Poor thing, to be in so much pain.*

"Listen, I know what we can do," I said. "Let's give my dad a call. He'll have good advice."

Dad was great. That afternoon, he made a three-way call with Amy and Jeff (who was working in Dallas) and tried to counsel them back together. It was obvious that their relationship was hanging by a thread. After ninety minutes of intense discussion, the three-way telephone conversation concluded.

"Do you hear what I'm hearing?" Dad asked Amy.

"Yes." She was getting it. Jeff was sending out strong signals that his career was more important to him than his marriage to or his love for her.

It ended up that later that evening, Dad and I boarded an American Airlines flight from Dallas to JFK. He described to me what had happened during the phone call, and that's when I decided to let 'er rip, to tell him about my real feelings for Amy. Dad was so touched that he was beside himself when I told him how much I liked her.

"But you can't tell anybody, Dad. It'll ruin the whole deal."

"I promise not to say anything. My lips are sealed," he said, as he made a zipperlike move across his lips.

"Dad, you're going to have to put some money on it." I know my father. He's the type of guy who *wanted* to be a male cheerleader just so he could yell family secrets through a megaphone.

"Okay, I'll pay you a thousand dollars if I say anything. Promise."

We weren't in New York more than an hour when Kathie Lee Gifford came over to me and said, "Wow, that is so cool that you like this Amy. I can't believe how romantic this story is."

I looked over at my father, who looked as though he had swallowed a canary. He shrugged his shoulders as if to say, *It wasn't my fault.* And I never did see the thousand dollars.

"Don't worry," said Kathy. "I'll sing at your wedding."

From New York, I flew on to Mazatlán to start my Spanish-intensive program.

**Amy:** A week or two after Michael left for Mazatlán, I was at the home of Jeff's parents. No one was there except Jeff and me, and we were having a talk in the living room.

Things were really getting tense between us. For months I had nursed a nagging feeling that all was not right between us. Each time Jeff and I began discussing our upcoming marriage, I could hear the hedging in his voice.

"Can you commit to December 3?" I asked.

"No, I can't at this time."

"Well, then, there's nothing else to be said," I said. "We've been dating for four years. If you don't know by now, you'll never know."

"How can you say that?" he demanded. "Besides, if you don't marry me, it's going to take you two, three years to cultivate a relationship with another guy before you'll know whether you'll marry him."

"You don't know that. We don't know what the future holds. What I do know is that if you don't know whether you're ready, then there is a problem." That's when I shut down. "You know what? This is not meant to be." I took off the ring and handed it to him.

I drove to my parents' home outside of Houston, tears rolling down my cheeks. I fell onto my bed and sobbed. It was over—more than four years up in smoke. What would my friends think? I needed someone I could talk to, someone I could trust. Someone like Michael Smalley.

**Michael:** As you can imagine, while I was in Mexico, Amy was in nearly every waking thought. Since I was here and she was there and we couldn't communicate, I had to rely on the Lord to see what would happen. There was no IM or MySpace.com in those days.

I vividly remember God saying, *You need to send her a letter—a letter to uplift her and tell her how much you appreciate her.*

*Oh, I get it, Lord. One of those "love bombardment" letters, kind of like when kids get in a circle and say something nice about the person in the center.* I thought of all her good qualities and personality traits and made a list.

I labored over a long letter that praised Amy to the hilt, encouraging her to stick close to the Lord and reminding her that God had a wonderful plan for her life. I can remember writing, "You are so special, and the person who marries you will be the luckiest guy in the world."

**Amy:** Michael's letter was waiting for me in the mailbox after I got home from the emotional breakup and handing back the engagement ring.

What an awesome letter—I still cherish it today! Each sentence was filled with love and encouragement. My heart melted, not for Michael, because that's not where my focus was, but for the Lord—that He would use Michael to send me a special letter at just the moment I needed it.

Over the next few weeks after the breakup, I continued to pray and seek God's guidance in everything. When I did, Michael's name and face kept coming to me. When I asked God what that was all about, He reminded me to be patient.

So I decided to chill out for a while.

**Think About It**

**Talk About It**

- Some have called falling in love temporary insanity! What have you found to be both the *incredible* and *frustrating* feelings that come with a meltdown over a special person who's come into your life?
- Why do you find it easy or not so easy to trust God with the process of finding a spouse?
- What is your plan for when the tingly feelings inevitably wear off?

# The Five Most Important Compatibility Issues

**M**ichael: We'll tell you more about our love story as we continue this book, but when it suddenly dawned on Amy that she and Jeff had divergent ideas on religion and how they related to God, that was the beginning of the end. The fact that she was a Southern Baptist and he was a Roman Catholic made for some stark differences in their worldviews regarding what they believed about God and how they worshiped Him. Those spiritual differences didn't make Jeff a bad person or Amy closer to God, but when push came to shove, Amy realized that she would be giving up a great deal of who she was to marry Jeff. That's when Amy realized how important her spiritual heritage was to her.

Amy wouldn't find out until years later when she earned her master's degree in marriage and family counseling that spiritual incompatibility is a major predictor of divorce. In fact, conflict over spiritual beliefs is part of a baker's dozen of significant issues that couples must be on the same page about going into marriage, according to Dr. David Olson.

**Amy:** I mentioned Dr. Olson in chapter 1. Now a retired University of Minnesota professor, Dr. Olson is known for developing the first and most widely used premarital assessment called Premarital Preparation and Relationship Enhancement, or PREPARE/ENRICH. Although it's been around for about twenty-five years, it wasn't until the mid-1990s that PREPARE became the standard tool of measurement in premarital counseling, assessing twenty areas of a couple's relationship. (Another premarital tool called FOCCUS is also very good.) In PREPARE/ENRICH, you're asked if you agree or disagree with nearly two hundred statements, such as:

- "When we are having a problem, my partner often gives me the silent treatment."
- "My partner and I are best friends and lovers."
- "My partner has some personality characteristics or habits I do not like."
- "I can easily share my positive and negative feelings with my partner."
- "I am very satisfied with the amount of affection I receive from my partner."
- "We have similar styles of spending and saving."
- "Sometimes I wish my partner was more careful about spending money."
- "Some relatives or friends have concerns about our upcoming marriage."

- "I have some concerns about how my partner will be as a parent."
- "Household tasks will be equally shared by us."
- "We sometimes disagree on how we should practice our religious beliefs."[1]

That last statement would have been one that a counselor would have zeroed in on if Jeff and I had participated in a PREPARE/ENRICH assessment. It's questions like these that unearth feelings and beliefs that usually remain buried during the dating period. The answers to these statements are used to show young couples how compatible they *really* are—or aren't. PREPARE/ENRICH is an astonishingly accurate predictor of divorce, and the information it uncovers results in 10–20 percent of participating couples breaking off their engagements. Everyone is better off when that happens, except for the florist and the caterer, of course.

When a PREPARE/ENRICH evaluation raises red flags, neither Michael nor I blow the hand-holding couple out of the water and tell them they shouldn't get married. Instead, we try to show them that they have serious incompatibility issues. "Look, let me outline this for you," I will say. "I highly recommend that you get these things fixed, because if you don't, there's a very strong chance that you will get divorced."

I usually have their undivided attention then. Next, I walk them through their weaknesses (as well as their strengths), painstakingly paying attention to their relational weak spots: gender roles, sex-pectations, when they will try to have children, and how they plan to spend the money they earn. The time to talk through these issues is before the marriage. Imagine the shock of a young woman who gets married and begins looking for a job in a new city only to find that her husband has designs for her staying home all day, baking cookies and cleaning house.

"I'm going to find myself a job," she says.

"Oh no, you're not," he replies. "No wife of mine is going to work. Your job is to raise the children, and the sooner we have kids, the better!"

"Is that so? Why don't you see what happens when you try to come within ten feet of me, mister!"

I'd say they have a little situation on their hands. That's why Michael and I pay close attention to the PREPARE/ENRICH results, looking for these divorce predictors. We explain that there is no perfect match in the game of love, no matter how many glowing testimonials they hear from star-ry-eyed couples who met through online dating services and are now married. "Idealizing a mate is a recipe for headache and heartache," said James Houran, PhD, a clinical psychologist who has worked as a therapist and personality researcher. "So is the belief that a compatibility test is the answer to your relationship prayers. Compatibility tests are simply tools to help you gain further insight into the temperament, personality, attitudes, and behavior of a prospect."[2]

## THE SIGNIFICANT ISSUES

Michael: At the end of the day, there are twelve significant issues that marriage-minded couples must talk through, according to Dr. Olson. They are:

1. Communication
2. Conflict Resolution
3. Personality Issues
4. Financial Management
5. Sexual Expectations

6. Role Relationship
7. Leisure Activities
8. Children and Parenting
9. Family and Friends
10. Marriage Expectations
11. Cohabitating Issues
12. Spiritual Beliefs[3]

Even this list is not exhaustive, but now let's take a closer look at what we think are the top five issues:

1. Spiritual Beliefs
2. Personality Issues
3. Financial Management
4. Children and Parenting
5. Sexual Expectations

## Spiritual Beliefs

Differences in religious practices and beliefs can create Grand Canyon–like fissures in a relationship. As we said before, that was the underlying reason why Amy and Jeff broke off their engagement. Imagine a Southern Baptist marrying a Catholic. The Southern Baptist is saying, *We go to church Wednesday nights, Sunday mornings, and Sunday nights, and we go to this brunch and that potluck,* while the Catholic is saying, *Fuggedaboutit. We're going to Mass on Sunday mornings.* That's a rather large difference in how much you see yourselves going to church.

The differences in spiritual practices get messier when you begin to think about which religion any children will be raised in. Amy naturally assumed that the kids would be raised in the Protestant tradition, while Jeff presumed that their children would be attending catechism and learning Catholic dogma.

Still, many couples sweep those differences under the rug. I'll never forget the time I was in Colorado Springs a day before one of our marriage seminars. I needed a haircut, so I walked into a salon and was shown a chair. A friendly woman, probably in her midthirties, asked me what kind of haircut I wanted. Within two sentences, I could tell that she had an accent.

"Where are you from?" I asked.

"Holland."

"Really? That's neat. How did you get here?"

"I got married." *Snip, snip.* "What are you doing here?" she asked.

"I'm in Colorado Springs to speak at a marriage conference."

"A marriage conference?"

"Well yes, I'm a marriage therapist."

The moment I said I was a marriage therapist, the floodgates opened. "Oh, I wish my husband would go to your marriage conference," she said, which I found interesting. *Why not herself?*

"Why? Are you struggling with something?"

"Well, we argue a lot, we're not getting along, and I'm thinking about leaving him."

"Do you have children?"

"Yes, we have two children. One is eight years old; the other is a few years younger."

"What's behind your problem?"

"Well, we have this difference in religion."

I'm thinking, *Okay, she must be talking about the differences between Protestants and Catholics. I see that a lot.*

"May I inquire what your differences are?"

"My husband is a Southern Baptist, and I'm a Wiccan."

*A Wiccan?* A Wiccan was a nice way of saying that she was a witch.

I was stunned. How on earth did those two ever get married? When I asked that question, in a diplomatic way, I learned that her husband was from Alabama, born with the southern culture in his blood, which included being raised in a Southern Baptist church. *How did this guy miss the whole witch thing? How was it possible that a couple got married and never even discussed that?*

When she finished cutting my hair, I gave her my card and invited her and her husband to attend the marriage conference as my treat, but I never saw either of them. I left Colorado Springs with a distinct feeling that their marriage was doomed unless she became a follower of Christ.

Spiritual incompatibility is important because you're dealing at a soul level that stirs up intense emotions as well as intense conflict. Here's the mistake that some people make: they think spiritual incompatibility is no big deal when they're dating. But what happens when the relationship turns serious and this hasn't been addressed? Well, the first thing that usually gets discussed after an engagement is, where do we get married?

Amy assumed that since the bride's family was footing the bill for the wedding, she would naturally get married in her home church, a Southern Baptist congregation. Yet Jeff grew up in the Roman Catholic tradition, where not marrying "in the church" meant that he might as well not get married at all, at least in the eyes of the Catholic Church.

If the differences in spiritual points of view don't hit soon after you marry, they will smack you when you have kids. What are you going to teach them about God? Where are they going to go to church? That's when spiritual incompatibility becomes a deep, personal battle that easily leads to divorce because there's no win-win in those types of situations.

I remember speaking at a seminar in Branson, Missouri, where a young woman, an eighteen-year-old high school senior, sat near the front. She raised her hand after I made this point on spiritual compatibility. "I totally disagree," she said. "For example, my boyfriend and I don't have any problems, and I'm a Catholic and he's a Mormon."

I cocked an eyebrow. "Are you serious?" I asked.

She blushed. "We've been together three years, and we're going to get married."

"Where do you think you'll get married?"

"I don't know. I haven't thought about it."

"Well, I can assure you that if you don't get married in a Catholic church, then the marriage won't be ordained. And the same goes for him. If you don't get married in a Mormon church, his family will feel the same way."

She looked at me like a deer caught in headlights.

**Amy:** A subset of spiritual values would be your political worldview (which is heavily shaped by your religious values). Even the secular world understands the need for couples to share the same cultural and political values, which makes it hard to understand how James Carville, a sharp-tongued defender of President Clinton and a Democratic Party operative, coexists in the same marriage with Mary Matalin, a sharp-tongued defender of President Bush and a Republican Party operative. But they have remained together since their marriage on Thanksgiving Day in 1993.

In the online world, you can go looking for your political soul mate. ConservativeMatch.com is for "sweethearts, not bleeding hearts." At the other end of the political spectrum, ActForLove.org was founded by "progressive activists" as a place to meet liberals, Democrats, and "folks who actually care about the world."

If you believe that women have the right to choose an abortion or you are in favor of Adam marrying Steve instead of Eve, then ActForLove.org and Liberalhearts.com is where you ought to be.

## Personality Issues

**Michael:** When online dating services send a list of wonderful people who are a compatibility match, couples who meet and move the relationship ball down the road often forget that even though they may have the same interests, they have unique personalities.

I'll have a lot more to say about personality types in our next chapter, but guys and gals basically fall under nine basic temperament types. Who you are, and the person you're interested in, are more than the sum of the neighborhood you grew up in, your educational background, and your ethnic heritage. The greatest impact upon your personality happened from the inborn traits that you inherited and that now subconsciously affect your behavior. These traits, passed through the genes you received from your parents, include intelligence, race, sex, and many other factors.

Dealing with personality traits and compatibility can get a little tricky. For example, concerning personality, you do not necessarily want someone who is exactly like you. Differences in personality are an important part of connecting with each other. At the same time, you do want to be able to understand each other and your differences. The divide should not be huge.

Amy and I are so different that we definitely would have flunked this part of any compatibility system. For instance, I'm fun-oriented, impulsive, relaxed, spontaneous, and crazy. Amy is the opposite! She is organized, detailed, analytical, fact-oriented, and intense. One of our biggest areas of contention over the years has been the extreme differences in our personalities. We find it hard to empathize with each other, but we're getting better at it after eleven years of marriage, if only because we've improved at allowing each other to be ourselves.

## Financial Management

**Amy:** Looking for fireworks? Watch a couple fight over how and on what they spend their money. After talking with couples, I have concluded that disagreement over money management places tremendous stress on a young marriage.

Online dating services, at least the ones I'm familiar with, don't ask if your college loans are paid up or how much credit card debt you're saddled with. People are naturally reticent about discussing money in any premarital situation, because it's either embarrassing or boasting, depending on the financial health of their bank accounts. This is one area that is best handled during a premarital counseling situation.

As Christians, we know money isn't the most important thing in life, but you would not know that by seeing how much couples fight over money—or the lack of it.

What I remind couples is that they're not fighting over money but rather over their ways of dealing with money. I'll ask questions like:

- "Are you a spender or saver?"
- "Do you like a balanced checkbook, or is your idea of balancing your checkbook accomplished by switching banks?"
- "What did your parents teach you about money?"

This latter question is particularly important to ask because the answers will reveal a lot about a couple's differences or similarities. You may not have liked what your parents did with their finances, but they were your major influence on handling money.

## Children and Parenting

**Michael:** It happens every time: When I ask a couple if they want children, they look at each other with longing eyes, as if they can't wait for those Kodak moments to happen. Then one will declare, "Yes, we want children."

Although Amy and I have counseled a handful of couples who said they preferred to remain childless, the desire to spring the next generation from the loins runs deep. I never attempt to dampen those wistful longings, but online dating services aren't designed to ask the tough questions like, will she work outside the home after the children come?

Fewer and fewer moms are having the option to stay at home with their children. If staying home is your goal, then you will have to be prepared to make sacrifices, such as living in a smaller home, driving older cars, and foregoing Disney World vacations. However, every couple we've met making this sacrifice said it was worth it.

Beyond the stay-at-home issue are things like discipline strategies, how many children you want to have, and how your children will be raised spiritually. World wars have been started over lesser things than a person's view on spanking versus time-outs. Some people have been raised in homes where they heard that spanking was a form of child abuse that ensured the child would grow up thinking that problems could be solved in a violent manner. Others were raised in homes where their parents fell asleep with Dr. James Dobson's *Dare to Discipline* on the nightstand, so they were the recipients of a well-placed thwack to the bottom when they misbehaved or tested their parents' authority.

## Sexual Expectations

As Gwyneth—the woman on the plane who told me about her one-night stand—learned to her sorrow, there are guys who view online dating as a way to bed more women. Their expectations are one-night flings with no emotional attachments.

Young men, because of their genetic hardwiring, have this gargantuan desire for sexual release—the more often, the better. Young women receive intimacy through relationship, communication, and tender, nonsexual acts like touching, sharing, and hugging, and they rarely have a matching level of desire for doing the wild thing.

In our sensuously charged culture, where boy-meets-girl-and-goes-right-to-bed-and-lives-happily-ever-after is a staple of today's entertainment shows, you would think that plenty of sex equals plenty of happiness. But all you have to do is be married for longer than two weeks to know that's not quite the case.

We'll say more about sex later—including the importance of staying out of bed until your marriage night—but for now, we're going to practice a form of coitus interruptus and ask that you wait until we unveil chapter 7, when we lift the covers on the topic of all things sexual.

## WHERE WE GO FROM HERE

**Amy:** I hope you understand that when it comes to meeting that special person, we're not saying that you should stay away from online dating sites or all the other places, from church to Starbucks, where singles meet one another. The point of *More Than a Match* is to help you discover and feel confident about what true love is and how you can ensure that your love lasts forever. Just finding the right person is not enough; in fact, that is the easy part. The reality is that it's not just about getting married but rather enjoying marriage to the fullest. Just meeting the right person will not accomplish this important goal of marriage.

**Michael:** If you're open to pursuing, or being pursued, then this is a step in life that should not be taken lightly. Before Amy and I ever got together, before we ever started dating and courting and all that mushy stuff, I prayed for Amy or whoever my future mate would be. I didn't want to get ahead of the Lord on such an important issue, which leads us to something you need to remember: the first step on the road to marriage is prayer.

**Amy:** When we give God control over our lives, we're free to trust in His bountiful grace and be confident that He knows who would be best suited for us in lifelong marriages. Nonetheless, He's given us brains so we can question that if a relationship seems too good to be true, it probably is too good to be true. For instance, I know that when some couples are introduced through an online dating service and sparks fly, it's natural to think that God ordained the match because of the incredible circumstances— and technology—that brought them together. It is pretty amazing to be matched with someone close in age who shares the same hobbies and leisure-time activities, as well as the same spiritual foundation. If that were to happen, how should you react?

By praying! Just because some computer says you're compatible with someone in twenty-nine different areas doesn't mean that you get a free pass. Take it to the Lord in prayer. Think it through as well. What are your long-term goals? What does this relationship mean to you? Is it for selfish reasons, such as enjoying guilt-free sex? Landing a trophy husband or trophy wife just so you can impress your sorority sisters or fraternity brothers?

Michael and I are great proponents of being intentional when it comes to finding that special person, and being intentional needs to happen before you fill out an online questionnaire or decide to join a singles' group at church. A great way to get intentional is to make a list of qualities you would like to see in a potential spouse. We'll describe some of those qualities in our next chapter.

## Think About It

## Talk About It

- Do you agree or disagree that there is no perfect match when it comes to finding a marriage partner? Explain your answer.
- These are the compatibility factors we think are the most crucial in making a good decision when selecting a mate: spiritual beliefs, personality issues, financial management, children and parenting, and sexual expectations.

   On which of these factors are you and your potential mate most compatible? Which are the factors that need more discussion and work?

   In addition to these, is there any other factor you feel you must consider as carefully?

# 5

# Your Top **Ten List**

Dear Tech Support:

Last year I upgraded from Boyfriend 5.0 to Husband 1.0 and noticed a slowdown in the performance of the flower and jewelry applications that had operated flawlessly under the Boyfriend 5.0 system.

In addition, Husband 1.0 uninstalled many other valuable programs, such as Romance 9.9, and installed undesirable programs such as NFL 7.4, NBA 3.2, and NHL 4.1.

Conversation 8.0 also no longer runs, and Housecleaning 2.6 simply crashes the system. I've tried running Nagging 5.3 to fix these problems, but to no avail. What can I do?

Signed,

Desperate

Dear Desperate:

First, keep in mind that Boyfriend 5.0 was an entertainment package, while Husband 1.0 is an operating system. Try to enter the command C:/ITHOUGHTYOULOVEDME and install Tears 6.2. Husband 1.0 should then automatically run the applications Guilt 3.3 and Flowers 7.5.

But remember, overuse can cause Husband 1.0 to default to such applications as Grumpy Silence 2.5, Reading Newspaper 7.0, or Watching Sitcoms 6.1. Please keep in mind that Watching Sitcoms 6.1 is an annoyingly disruptive program that will create SnoringLoudly.WAV files.

DO NOT install Mother-in-Law 1.0 or reinstall another Boyfriend program. These are not supported applications and will crash Husband 1.0. It could also potentially cause Husband 1.0 to default to the program Girlfriend 9.2, which runs in the background and has been known to introduce potentially serious viruses into the operating system.

In summary, Husband 1.0 is a great program, but it does have limited memory and can't learn new applications quickly. You might consider buying additional software to enhance its system perfor-mance. I personally recommend Marriage for a Lifetime Seminar 3.0 and Marital Intensive 4.5 combined with such applications as that old standby...Lingerie 5.9 (which has been credited with improved performance of its hardware).

Good luck,

Tech Support[1]

**Michael:** Ah, if only this thing called love could be as easy as a new software installation. Actually, relationships between the sexes are much more complicated than any sophisticated software program, including those running on giant mainframes behind the online dating services, because many people still haven't found—and really aren't sure—what they're looking for, to play off a Bono lyric.

In the quest to find that special someone, you need to be thinking intentionally about the qualities you would want to see in a potential mate. If guys put as much thought into what type of person they want to date and eventually marry as they put into researching their next set of wheels, there would be far fewer busted relationships and subsequent divorces. And if young women adopted a more calm and collected, eyes-wide-open approach, they wouldn't fall for the first hunk on the make.

There's another reason you want to think and act intentionally: decisions on whom you will date and subsequently marry last for life, and, thanks to longer life expectancies, you're going to be sharing a toothpaste tube with that person for decades. Did you know that if your marriage goes the distance, there's a strong chance you and your spouse will make it to your golden anniversary—fifty years? That's half a century! My mom and dad celebrated their fortieth anniversary in 2005, prompting Mom to state that it's been quite a journey.

**Amy:** Marriages that last longer than a silver anniversary are a fairly recent phenomenon in the course of human events. Back in 1900, couples could expect to live until their late forties, which meant they were fortunate to live long enough to see their last child marry and leave the home. Today, if you wed in your twenties, the actuary tables predict that you will live—if God grants you the years—a good twenty to twenty-five years *after* your last child has left the nest. (The average life expectancy for males is seventy-five years; for females, it's eighty years.)[2]

Thus, the decision regarding *whom* you will marry is not to be taken lightly. (I know, I sound like your parents.) The average man gets married at around age twenty-seven; the average woman at around age twenty-five. When you're transitioning out of school and into a career, you are setting the stage for how you will live the rest of your life. Life is so fresh in your twenties. You usually don't have heavy responsibilities yet—providing for a family, raising children, paying the mortgage each month, running a company, or meeting a payroll. You're not as set in your ways, at least compared to those in their thirties and older. You can get *used* to new settings and environments easier, and believe us, you'll be calling upon every ounce of flexibility after your wedding day.

Let's definitely talk about this, but in regards to when you might want to start having children, because things do get harder and more complicated the longer you wait. You also reach your physical peak in your twenties, usually around age twenty-six. Ask any young parent, especially mothers: you'll call upon every energy reserve you have once those babies arrive. We feel that what you lack in life experiences you more than make up for with your vitality.

Knowing that, there are two things you should do before you join an online dating service or allow your best friend to play matchmaker and set you up with a blind date. You should:

1. Sit down and think through a list of the top ten qualities that you'd like to see in a partner.
2. Discover what personality type you are, and when you meet that special person, explore how your two personality types mesh—or clash.

## THE TOP TEN QUALITIES

**Michael:** This is an important assignment. The next occasion you have some thinking time—toying around on your laptop during a long flight, sitting on a park bench, taking in a sunset—type in or write down some qualities in a potential mate that would be important to you.

There is one quality that must be on your list—in fact, we make it a nonnegotiable: if you are a Christian, then your future mate *must* be a Christian. The Bible is quite clear in 2 Corinthians 6:15, saying, "How can a believer be a partner with an unbeliever?" In the old King James Version, this was the infamous "be ye not unequally yoked" passage (see 2 Corinthians 6:14), referring to the wooden bar joining two draft animals (such as oxen) at the heads or necks for working in the field together.

Our knowledge of farm animals wouldn't fill a milk bucket, but if two different kinds of animals were yoked together to pull a plow, such as a donkey and an ox, you'd have a heap of trouble on your hands. The yoke would weigh heavily on one animal while choking the other, or the animal with the longer stride would painfully drag the other along by the neck. This is a great word picture of a pair unable to pull smoothly or painlessly together because they are not alike! Believe us, after you get married, you want to be in sync with your spouse in every way possible, especially in your spiritual walk, because marriage is hard work. Nor should you get involved with someone who you *think* could become a Christian. "A triple-braided cord is not easily broken," goes the proverb (Ecclesiastes 4:12), and the three strands refer to you, your spouse, and God.

**Amy:** As you begin to think about the qualities you would like to see in your future husband or wife, you have to be servant minded when you're thinking about marriage. If both sides are giving of themselves, then you will have what it takes to make a marriage go. You will be demonstrating to your spouse that you understand what servanthood and true love are all about. The love chapter of the Bible, 1 Corinthians 13, lists those servant qualities:

> Love is patient and kind. Love is not jealous or boastful or proud or rude. Love does not demand its own way. Love is not irritable, and it keeps no record of when it has been wronged. It is never glad about injustice but rejoices whenever the truth wins out. Love never gives up, never loses faith, is always hopeful, and endures through every circumstance....
>
> When I was a child, I spoke and thought and reasoned as a child does. But when I grew up, I put away childish things. Now we see things imperfectly as in a poor mirror, but then we will see everything with perfect clarity. All that I know now is partial and incomplete, but then I will know everything completely, just as God knows me now.
>
> There are three things that will endure—faith, hope, and love— and the greatest of these is love. (1 Corinthians 13:4–7, 11–13)

You are no longer a child when you marry. You must put away the childish things. You should be ready to love that other person with a servant heart, honoring him or her without any expectations in return. Now that takes maturity! It helps to feel secure in who you are in Christ as you move toward loving someone the unconditional way that Christ loves us.

Are you looking for others to fix or, as Tom Cruise's character Jerry Maguire once said, "complete" you? That may work in the movies but not in real life. If you aren't emotionally healthy, your natural response will be to depend on your spouse to make you happy, which can leave you powerless and unfulfilled.

Now that we've established these important principles, let's discuss the rest of the qualities that you may want to see in a potential mate. Several of these could be part of your list.

## Qualities That Would Be Good in a Guy

**He comes from a good family.** The environment in which your future husband was raised is huge. This is not to say that someone raised by a single-parent mom can't become a great husband. What this is saying is that someone raised in a loving, two-parent household has a greater chance of being a good husband because he had *role models*. He witnessed (hopefully) a father who loved and sacrificed for his family.

**He acts like he'd make a great father.** Have you seen him interact with nieces and nephews? Does he like lifting little kids and making them squeal?

**He has a heart for people.** Is he a kind person? How does he treat others in your presence? Is he nice to and respectful of his mother? The way he treats his mother will often predict the way he will treat you. What about others? Is he rude to "lowly" waitresses? Does he look down on parking attendants? Or does he have a great heart for others?

**He is honest.** Can you trust that he means what he says and says what he means? Do you catch him telling little white lies to not upset you?

**He has a cheerful heart.** Is he moody? the silent type? You want someone to be a kick to be around. Can you tease him without him getting irritated?

**He has a sense of humor.** Does he make you laugh? Or is he as dull as watching paint dry? Can you make him laugh?

**He's accepting of who you are.** Some guys like to beat around the bush, like making asides about weight ("Still packing the freshman fifteen?") or a "different" family member ("That Uncle Ed of yours is a real fruit loop").

**He seems to be compatible with your family.** They aren't kidding when they say that when you marry someone, you marry his family as well. So flip that around: when he marries you, he's marrying your family. How does he get along with your parents and siblings? Is he looking at his watch, wondering when the torture will end, or does he cheerfully interact with your family?

**He knows who he is, and he knows where he's going.** Does he convey a winner's attitude? You want a guy who exudes confidence that says, *Hey, I know where I'm going in life, and if you want to hitch your wagon up with mine...*

**He is not the jealous type.** Jealousy is often a sign of lack of trust.

**He's willing to wait.** Sure, the hormones are cranked as high as they will go, but is he pressuring you into bed? Is he spouting the same old lines to weaken your resolve ("Don't you love me?" or "You're the only one for me")? Is he constantly pawing you?

**He's attractive.** Sure, a gorgeous hunk with killer abs and a full head of hair counts for something, but Jude Law–like looks are fleeting. (I can't believe I just wrote that.) Still, it's okay to look for someone who attracts you physically. Realize, though, that physical looks are only one part of the combination plate, not the whole enchilada.

**He's on the same page as you.** Do you fight over politics? Are your attitudes toward faith similar? Is he a spender or a saver? Does he believe in spanking children at the appropriate time, or does he prefer to put children in time-out?

**He appreciates your role.** Will he support you if you plan to work full time? If you decide to stay at home, will he see you as lazy?

**He values his faith.** Does he actively participate in worship, or do you have to drag him with you to church?

**He doesn't mind watching chick-flick movies.** Some guys could watch *Dumb and Dumber* seven days a week and twice on Sunday, but would he enjoy watching a well-crafted love story with you?

## Qualities That Would Be Good in a Gal

**She values her faith.** Does she turn to the Bible for encouragement and teaching? Would she attend a couples' Bible study with you?

**She has a great personality.** Do you find her fun to be around? Or are you walking on eggshells? Does she seem to need to be around you all the time, or can she be alone and enjoy herself?

**She is honest.** Can you trust her to tell the truth even when it's difficult?

**She is cute as a button and sexy as a Hawaiian sunset.** Is she beautiful to you? Can you tell your friends that you're in love with the most beautiful woman in the world? Do you get a little fuzzy when you kiss?

**She has intelligence and is not afraid to use it.** You're going to be building a family and a lifetime of memories. Can she hold up her end of an intellectual conversation?

**She wants to be a mom someday.** If you're thinking about bringing children into this world, then you want to meet someone who has a nurturing personality. Some women are more career-minded these days. That's fine, but if both of you are looking forward to parenthood, you'll have to talk through how children will change career goals.

**She reaches out to others.** Is she an introvert or extrovert? Maybe you would prefer someone with a more cozy personality who wants to cocoon at home with you. But some men prefer a woman who is the life of the party.

**She complements your weaknesses.** Perhaps you're the most disorganized person in the world, but she loves to keep a tidy house. Will she cut you some slack and pick up after you?

**She respects herself.** Maybe someone who establishes clear physical boundaries up front in the relationship is the type of person you need to help you stay pure.

**She likes action movies.** You don't want to spend the rest of your life watching those syrupy chick-flick movies, do you? You want someone who appreciates the artistry behind car chases and gun shootouts.

After I had broken off my engagement to Jeff, I decided that the next time I met someone with possibilities, a failed relationship was not going to happen again. Believe it or not, I had been writing down my own top ten qualities since I was in junior high. I dug out my list, and at the top was an item called spiritual compatibility. For five years, I had tried to put Jeff into a box—my spiritual box. The fact that he was a Catholic didn't make him a bad person—far from it. It was just that my Southern Baptist upbringing meant that we had different ideas about how we related to God. Those differences meant that I found myself giving up more and more of who I was just to be with him. At the end of the day, I realized how important my spiritual heritage was to me.

Had I been checking my list and been honest with myself, I wouldn't have taken the relationship as far as I did. But I didn't know at the time that differences in religion were a major predictor of divorce. When I began getting serious with Michael, I soon found out that we were on the same page when it came to spiritual matters. I can't tell you how much that meant to me.

After overcoming that hurdle, I looked at number two on my list, which reminded me that I wanted to marry someone who had clear direction in his life. Did Michael know where he was going?

Early in our dating relationship, Michael made it clear to me that he would pursue counseling as a career. But if he had said a month later, "You know, counseling isn't all that it's cracked up to be. I think I want to become an airline pilot," that would have made me feel unstable about my future because Michael had been talking about going to graduate school and becoming a counselor. If he had suddenly tossed that career goal overboard so that we could move near a flight school, that would have unnerved me. I like stability and knowing where I'm going.

You will too, once you give a Top Ten Qualities List some thought. You definitely want to keep those qualities in the back of your mind, because when love happens, things move quickly.

## It's All in Your Personality Types

**Michael:** I am a fun-loving adrenaline junkie who likes to get crazy every now and then. That means I wanted to marry someone who wouldn't be fearful kayaking down a roaring, spring-fed river, someone who liked flying in a single-engine plane, going up in a hot-air balloon, or climbing sandstone spires in Moab, Utah. I certainly did not want a fearful wife who wouldn't allow our children to jump off a cliff with me into a lake or let Junior play football because he might get hurt. I knew that Amy was not the fearful type. Her ability to stand before tens of thousands of screaming football fans at Baylor, performing stunts and leading cheers, told me she was fearless. I found that part of Amy's personality exciting.

That's why you need to consider what kind of person you want to marry, the personality he or she should have. I travel around the world teaching on personalities, and here's what I say to audiences: through the years, some academics in psychology narrowed down human behavior, or temperament, into four basic types: sanguine, choleric, melancholy, and phlegmatic. Are you thinking, *Say what?* I'll explain.

Your personality is a combination of inborn traits that subconsciously affect your behavior, but one of those four aforementioned types usually predominates. Keep in mind that these traits are passed on by the genes, but you have to add intelligence, race, sex, and other factors to the mix.

The four descriptions—sanguine, choleric, melancholy, and phlegmatic—are terms developed centuries ago by the father of medicine, the Greek doctor Hippocrates. I would bet you a gyro sandwich that not one person in a thousand could tell you what a sanguine person is like or the characteristics of a phlegmatic person. (For the record, sanguines are fun-loving extroverts, while phlegmatics are organized and serious individuals. Here's a bit of trivia: the term *phlegmatic* comes from the Latin root *phlegm,* or mucus. That's right. Someone actually named a type of person after a bodily fluid, and one of the more gross ones at that!)

Some of the biggest matchmaking sites on the Internet tout their personality profiles as a way to draw you in ("A $50 Value!" and "Yours for Free!"). I've taken a lot of these personality assessments over the years, including the Myers-Briggs and the DiSC profiles. But the *best* personality profile assessment I've come across was developed by David Swift, PhD, whom I had the privilege of working with while at my dad's ministry in Branson.

Dr. Swift's system is based on a personality system called the Enneagram, which suggests that there are nine basic personality types in human nature. These nine were developed by an eccentric teacher named George Gurdjieff at the beginning of the twentieth century and expanded upon by scholars and authors Don Riso and Russ Hudson in recent years.

Dr. Swift teamed up with my father and a slew of psychological experts to develop an assessment tool called the Personality Profile for Couples, which helps you discover who you are as a potential mate and gives couples the ability to decipher their unique personalities while highlighting their strengths and blind spots.[3]

Every couple should take this profile! (To order a CD that you can plug into your computer to complete the assessment, check out www.thesmalley store.com.) What's cool is that you get two complete personality profile tests (each nine pages long), immediate evaluation upon completion, and nine pages of results describing your personality style and how it responds in relationships. *The Personality Profile for Couples CD* will instantly let you know your strengths and areas of need as you relate as a couple.

When I first took this test, the results blew my mind, because when I'd taken the basic personality profiles that you find on online dating sites, I always ended up testing with the exact same personality type as my father. But when we took Dr. Swift's test, my dad came out as a three and I came out as a seven. I'll explain below what these numbers indicate, but this result meant that Dad and I weren't peas in a pod—we were actually quite different! And after reading this personality profile for the first time, I almost freaked out. It was like Dr. Swift had been living in my home my whole life, that's how accurate it was.

Here are Dr. Swift's nine basic types, followed by brief descriptions:

1. **Reformer:** "I do everything the right way." These people have high standards for themselves and others. They love to get things

right the first time and be thorough in all they do. They love to follow rules and are realistic about life and relationships.

2. **Helper:** "I must help others." Riso and Hudson say that twos are empathetic, compassionate, and full of feelings for others. They're people who love people, the good Samaritan types who are joyful, nurturing, gracious, patient, kind, merciful, and forgiving—all the good stuff in 1 Corinthians 13.

3. **Motivator:** "I need to succeed." These people are highly motivated to succeed and win in life. They often care what other people think of them, but they remain self-assured and goal oriented.

4. **Romantic:** "I am special." These are the actors and lovers of the world, the creative types. They have sensitive feelings and tend to be friendly and aware.

5. **Thinker:** "I want to understand everything." These are the introverts who prefer solitude. Silence and meditation can often be very soothing to a five. They are analytical and insightful.

6. **Questioners:** "I am affectionate and skeptical." These people are loyal and definitely like to question everything, including the motives behind people's actions. They can be suspicious of things and tend to see the cup as half-empty, but they are responsible as well.

7. **Adventurer:** "I am happy and open to new things." These guys, and the gals too, just want to have fun. Sevens are totally into adrenaline and action just for the pure energy of it all.

8. **Leader:** "I must be strong." These are the generals, captains, and presidents. They love to be in control and are intense problem-solvers. They are direct, confrontational, and self-confident.

9. **Peacemaker:** "I am at peace." These people love to be supportive and agreeable. They are receptive to people and are basically good-natured toward others and circumstances.[4]

In their book *The Enneagram Made Easy,* Renee Baron and Elizabeth Wagele give a great example of all the personality types and what they might say before a dinner party:

1. I hope I'm bringing the appropriate wine.
2. I hope my friends will all like each other.
3. I hope to do a lot of networking tonight.
4. I'm not in the mood for a party.
5. I wish I could stay home with my book on Lepidoptera, which is a large order of insects comprising the butterflies, moths, and skippers that as adults have four lanceolate, or broad, wings usually covered with brightly colored scales.
6. I wonder if Susan only invited me because she felt she had to.
7. If it isn't a fun group, I have other things in mind.
8. I'm going to give someone a piece of my mind tonight!
9. I'll feel so good if I make a nice connection tonight.[5]

Amy has a few one characteristics, but her strongest type is an eight, which makes her strong and independent, something I was definitely looking for. Cleanliness was also huge on her list, showing her one characteristics, so when she cleans the car, she really likes to detail it out. I'm talking about using Q-tips on the air conditioning vents—that type of clean.

As for me, a seven, my idea of cleaning the car is making a quick pass through the car wash and air drying the car by driving fast on the highway with the wind blowing in my hair. So you can imagine what happened after we got married and Amy learned a few things about me, including the way

I shed clothes from the moment I stepped through the front door and continued to drop sweaters and shirts all the way to the master bathroom. That drove her nuts.

Back then, I didn't see what the big deal was, nor could I believe how analytical she could be. One time, we watched a friend give his fiancée an engagement present—an impressionist lithograph. We were standing there admiring this thoughtful gift when Amy leaned over and whispered in my ear, "There are only eleven roses." I cracked up. Who but Amy would count the number of roses in a painting? Who cared if there weren't an even dozen?

I also learned quickly how Amy handled conflict differently than I did. She wanted to get the facts out so that she could process the information. While her communication style was two-way, my communication style was one-way, because I wanted her to buy in to what I was saying.

Even though we both *knew* we were different, we *still* had major adjustments to make in our first year of marriage. My indifferent attitude to clutter, dirty floors, and scattered clothes grated on Amy's nerves. I didn't like it when she harped on me to clean up; Her nitpicking caused me to cringe. It was like going to a party, but you couldn't have fun because you were so busy cleaning up after everyone else.

For my part, I needed to make changes in my cleanliness because that would honor Amy. So I became more attentive about keeping my dirty clothes off the floor, and when we built a house several years into our marriage, we made sure that it had two large, walk-in closets. If I was going to toss clothes on the floor, then I could at least do it in the walk-in closet and close the door to the mess.

## WHAT ARE YOU LIKE?

**Amy:** Learning about individual qualities will help us better understand each other and help us communicate more openly with others. Before you go on another date, order the Personality Profile for Couples CD at www.amyandmichael.org and take the test. Just remember: there are no right or wrong answers. Try to think of yourself in general terms and, if possible, outside of your relationship with your partner. Just enjoy the process and don't worry about how it turns out.

Discovering your personality tendencies will show you your strengths and weaknesses. And understanding the strengths and weaknesses of that special person in your life should help you relate to him or her better—and understand your differences better. Get feedback from family and friends, too, asking them if they think this personality description fits you.

Being different from each other helps a couple balance their relationship. Yes, you can be compatible when you have different personality types, but those differences should work to make you stronger, not weaker. *Understanding* what those personality tendencies are helps you see the value in them.

**Michael:** I'll never forget when Amy and I first started dating. Like so many love-struck couples, we each thought the other could do no wrong. If I forgot to bring my wallet to a restaurant, Amy would say, "Oh, that's so cute," as she reached into her purse to cover the meal. Once we married, however, Amy's viewpoint changed on those occasions when I didn't have my wallet at a restaurant. I think she used the word *irresponsible*, and it wasn't said in a nice way.

That's the difference between dating, which offers an emotional breather back home in between times together, and the nonstop, 24/7 aspect of marriage, where the two of you are together—or on each other's nerves—around the clock.

If you're in a relationship, you may reach a point where you're getting on each other's nerves. Or perhaps your personalities don't mesh as you once thought.

So what do you do if things are not working out? We'll discuss that topic, as well as the dating game, in our next chapter.

## Think About It

## Talk About It

- Okay, it's time to go to work! Pull out your laptop or find a pad of paper and write down your list of the top ten qualities you want in a lifelong marriage mate. Pray about this, take some time, have fun dreaming, and give it your best shot.
- Based on the brief descriptions we gave in this chapter, what personality type(s) do you think you are? What about your special friend—what are hers or his? Do you agree with the other person's evaluation of his or her personality? Enjoy the discussion!
- What specific areas of your personality would you like to work on?

# The Dating Game—Beginning and Ending a Relationship

**M**ichael: Where's a good place to meet Christian guys and ladies? The clichéd answer is church, but there's a time-honored reason for that: churches have always been great places to connect with people sharing the same spiritual values as you. The danger is that the church's singles' ministry can become a socially acceptable meat market, so you have to find a singles' ministry that really is a ministry.

The easiest time to meet people to date is when you're in college. It gets harder after you graduate; there's no way around that. If you're out of college, don't feel like the situation is hopeless, because unless you're on the ten-year plan, most people are out of college by the time they get married.

Of course, it's possible to meet someone where you work, but that's usually hit or miss unless you're working for a Christian organization. Either way, don't expect a big social life—at least compared to college—when you're holding down a job.

This explains why we've seen the rise of eHarmony.com and other Christian online dating sites; it's becoming increasingly difficulty to find someone compatible—there's the "C word" again—during the postcollege years. The ocean of people waiting for you in cyberspace is considerably larger than the pool of those available in a young single adults Sunday school class or at your place of employment.

**Amy:** Speed dating is another form of boy-meets-girl that has become popular. In speed dating, a group of singles gathers at a cafe or similar venue. Armed with name tags, scorecards, and their sparkling personalities, couples meet for seven minutes, during which they are allowed to discuss anything except their careers and where they live. Then a bell is rung, and the men move on to meet their next "date." Think of it as a flirt's version of musical chairs.

Following each seven-minute encounter, participants mark on cards whether they would have an interest in meeting any of their dates again. If a mutual interest is noted, speed dating organizers provide each person with the other's phone number.

Speed dating sounds like frenetic fun, but a sense of desperation hovers in the air, as if participants are trying to force something to happen. I wonder how confident a person you would meet at a speed date. Are participants really comfortable being single?

If you're among the postcollege crowd, be aware that if you're not happy being single, there's a good chance you won't be happy when you're married. Don't forget that feelings of desperation are like blood in the water; you're likely to attract predators with dishonorable intentions, as Gwyneth, the Manhattan young woman, learned to her sorrow.

That's not the way you want to start a dating relationship.

## WE'RE PRO-DATING

**Michael:** Amy and I share the philosophy that dating is a good thing, even for teens in high school (although we'd like to see more group dating with that age group). When you're in the latter years of college or on your own in your twenties, however, we believe that you shouldn't date the same person steadily until you feel you've met your future spouse and are ready to date with the intention of marriage.

When I was in my junior year of college, I was ready to seriously date, and when I heard that Amy had broken off her engagement, I was looking for something a lot more meaningful than a speed date.

That May afternoon I drove to Amy's apartment expecting to say good-bye forever, I was stunned when she hugged me fiercely after she answered the door. She threw her arms around my neck because she had just broken off her relationship with Jeff. I hugged her just as fiercely because we were like brother and sister at the time. But when I let go, she held on. The next thing I knew she was sobbing onto my shoulder.

I asked what any man would ask at this point when a woman is crying, "Is something wrong?"

*Duh! She's crying, you idiot.*

That's when Amy told me she had just broken off her engagement, and while she was bawling her little eyes out, I had to wipe a smile off my face.

I could not believe what I was hearing. The woman of my dreams had finally seen the light and ended her relationship, and I was the first single male to hear that good news!

But at that moment God did something powerful in my heart—this is what I heard Him say: *If you even think of moving in on Amy right now, I will destroy your children and your children's children!*

So instead of telling Amy how much I loved her, I decided to help her in her time of need. I escorted her to a nearby mall and bought all of my dad's marriage and relationship books for her, and I even went as far as to set up a conference call with her, Jeff, and my dad. Today, we joke that my father's first conversation with his future daughter-in-law was counseling her about her relationship with another man, but I digress.

Now before you start a campaign to have me sainted, let me be honest about why I set up that conference call with my father. I knew that if anyone could destroy what remained of their relationship, it was my father! (Okay, I'm kidding again, but I always like saying that.)

Even though my father's celebrated counseling skills couldn't save Amy and Jeff's engagement, I had to play my emotions close to the vest. I couldn't act too happy since breaking up had to be a traumatic event for Amy. "Wouldn't be prudent," as Dana Carvey would say when he was imitating President Bush (Dubya's father) on *Saturday Night Live.* My situation was helped when I had to take off for my summer term in Mexico to learn Spanish. From afar, I made myself available as a sounding board to Amy and penned lovesick poetry on the beaches of Mazatlán.

Nonetheless, I had been presented with a huge opportunity. The girl of my dreams was suddenly available. That meant I had a chance.

**Amy:** Two weeks after the breakup, word hit the streets in my hometown of Conroe, Texas, that I was available. I think I went out four times until I began dating this guy named Rob exclusively. I know what you're thinking: wasn't that awfully fast to start dating again after four years with another guy? Yes, it was, which goes to show you that I was on the rebound, although I didn't recognize it at the time.

On paper, Rob and I looked to be a great match. He was also from Conroe and had been a yell leader at Sam Houston State. And it didn't hurt matters that he was a good-looking guy with a great build—and was a committed Christian to boot.

I could tell Rob really wanted to pursue a relationship with me, but I kept thinking about Michael in Mexico and how sweet and caring he was. Something deep down told me that Michael Smalley was someone special, someone I needed to get to know better. That meant clearing the decks and cutting off all romantic ties so that I could focus on Michael. Could Michael and I have a serious relationship?

I remember having an intense discussion with Rob when Michael's name came up.

"Why in the world would you want to see Michael? What does he have that I don't have?" Rob asked.

"I can't put my finger on it right now, but I've been praying about it. The only thing that comes to my mind, and I know it sounds crazy, is that I see us ministering together. It's strange, I know, but I see myself speaking to women. I don't know if that will come true, but I want to find out."

I said this before Michael and I ever dated a single time.

I didn't know, though, if Michael would ask me out. At that point in my life, I didn't want to play around. I didn't want to be dating just to be dating or having fun. I wanted a relationship that was going to last.

**Michael:** I was able to call Amy from Mazatlán a few times during my summer Spanish program, and I could tell her heart was softening toward me. Talking on the telephone to her for more than an hour one time seemed a good indication she was interested in me, and I was already interested in her. After my Spanish course, I flew home to Branson in the middle of July.

She called my house the next morning, knowing that I should have gotten back to the States. The funny part is that when Amy called, I was in my parents' bathroom taking care of business. Mom and Dad had installed a phone in their throne room, and I instinctively picked up the phone when it rang. When I heard the voice on the other end, I freaked out. I mean, I couldn't hang up on Amy! Man, was that embarrassing, carrying on a conversation while trying to keep the noise down!

Anyway, I told her about how excited I felt being on U.S. soil again and how Branson was hopping in the summer with all the tourists in town to see acts like Glen Campbell and Yakov Smirnoff. During a lull in the conversation, I blurted out, "It's so much fun here. You need to come up sometime and see Branson."

"Yeah, I should do that," Amy said, which was all the encouragement I needed.

"Listen, my parents have all these frequent-flier miles. We could get you a ticket."

I expected Amy to hesitate, to think through what she would say next. I had opened a door into my heart. Would she slam it shut or walk on through?

"That sounds like fun. I'd love to come to Branson. How does next weekend sound?"

*She wants to come see me next weekend?*

**Amy:** I think my response caught Michael off guard, but I was ready to see whether this would work. In my heart and my mind and my prayers, he kept popping up. I wanted to focus on him and see what could develop.

"Next weekend?" Michael said. "Okaaay, that sounds great. Let me check with Mom, and I'll get back to you."

I drove home and called my mom to tell her that it looked as though I was flying to Branson to see Michael Smalley. Mom nearly dropped the cast-iron pan she was drying.

"*What* Michael?" She knew him, vaguely, from the Baylor yell team. "You mean Michael from Baylor?"

"Mom, this guy has been on my heart and my mind every time I've prayed about whom I will marry. I've made out this list with ten qualities I'm looking for, and this guy has all of them."

When I boarded a plane on Friday, July 19, Mom and her friend, Cindy, were praying for me and my budding relationship.

I was nervous and apprehensive on the flight to Springfield, Missouri. I wasn't sure if I could have romantic feelings for someone I'd known like a brother for so long. Oh well. I'd soon find out.

As I stepped off the plane that evening, Michael was standing in the Jetway holding a solitary yellow rose. (Back in those pre–September 11 days, they let you do things like that in small airports like Springfield-Branson National Airport.) He looked buff! Michael was tan, his muscles were bulging, and he looked great in a yellow shirt with a Mexican vest, something he obviously had picked up in Mazatlán.

I ran into his arms and gave him a big hug, which knocked the flower off its stem.

"Oh, that was your 'Welcome to Missouri' rose," he said as he handed me the rose stem.

"Sorry about that," I grinned.

I felt it! Right then I knew that this could work.

When I met Michael's dad, he was exactly where Michael said he would be—lounging on his recliner, fast asleep with the Weather Channel blaring in the background. Gary couldn't have been nicer or more charming. He reminded me of Michael—full of fun, a nonstop storyteller, and someone genuinely interested in what I had to say.

The following morning I met Michael's mom, Norma. I was pleased with our introductory "hi hello" meeting, and then Michael and I took a tour of Branson, stopping by Kanakuk Kamp, a Christian sports camp, where I met some of Michael's friends. They all seemed like quality Christian people. That evening, his parents invited us to dinner at the Candlestick Inn, one of Branson's finer restaurants. That would be my official meet-the-parents event.

After the salads were served, I heard Norma remark, "So, Amy, I hear you've had a hard summer. What was that like?"

*Oh no! She knows everything!*

I tried to stay composed. The thought came to my mind that she was testing me, to see whether I would rise to the occasion. Would I fall apart in a jumble of tears? "Yes, it's been a really rough summer," I confided, and from there, I told my story with openness. When I was done, full of emotion, I excused myself to the ladies' room.

**Michael:** As soon as Amy left the table, Mom leaned over to me and said, "Don't let this one get away."

*Oh my!* That was Mom talking, a mother who had never gotten excited about anybody I'd dated before. Dad was always the opposite. Even back in middle school, he would say, "Wow! You're interested in this new girl? Cool! Let's have a barbecue or have her over for a swim. We would love to meet her."

Now I was twenty-one years old, entering my senior year of college, and finally my parents were on the same page with me. Amy returned from her visit to the powder room.

"What do you want to do for the next few days?" my mother asked Amy.

"Get to know your son," she replied enthusiastically, which prompted a nervous laugh from everyone.

My parents had nothing to worry about. Amy and I had dated other people a great deal before settling down in our engagement, and that is something we felt comfortable with because we had each dated since our high school days. Dating can be controversial in some quarters, and I know I may take some flack because on this hot topic, the viewpoints run the gamut.

Some say that it doesn't make sense training for a long-term marriage with a series of short-term dating relationships. They say that when you date, you give a part of your heart to that person, a part that can never be reclaimed.

Amy and I have a different perspective. Dating, like nearly everything in life, has the capacity for good and evil. We, along with millions of others, have had extremely positive experiences in our dating relationships. We also checked into heartbreak hotel a few times. Does that mean that dating was bad? No! Neither was it sinful or evil.

Dating can help you find a spouse. If you never date anyone, how can you know who is the right one for you? Dating gives you the chance to experience someone in a closer manner. Dating is your opportunity to have a relatively emotionally intimate relationship with someone before you commit to a lifetime of marriage. The great developmental psychologist Dr. Erik Erikson believed that having romantic experiences (or dating) plays an important role in helping a person develop a personal identity and intimacy. He felt that dating shapes the course of future romantic relationships and marriage.

Our key argument is, "Look, if you follow the model of honoring yourself and honoring others, you're going to be okay." Ultimately, as you mature, you're going to make fewer mistakes. You're going to hurt people less. And, hurting isn't all bad if it's experienced in the right way. If you break up with a guy or girl, that will hurt. But finding a quality life is not about avoiding pain. That just can't be done.

Part of honoring the person you're involved with is watching what you say. My mom gave me some great advice when I was in high school. I was starting to seriously date a young woman named Stacey. Mom said, "Be careful about saying 'I love you.'"

My parents helped me understand the significance of the word *love* and how you don't want to throw it around. Overusing the word *love*, they said, guarantees that it will not actually stand for anything significant. Throughout the years I dated Stacey, I didn't tell her I loved her, and she didn't tell me either. That was one way to guard our hearts because, let's face it, very few dating relationships make it all the way to the altar. More often than not, the online match doesn't compute or the person you've been seeing ends up not being The One.

## WHEN IT'S NOT WORKING OUT

You and a lovely woman go out on a few dates, which means you've gotten to know each other better. Now some red flags are flapping in the breeze. For instance, she wonders why the quarterback doesn't just kick the ball into the end zone, and she has never set foot inside a Mexican restaurant. She doesn't believe in shaving her legs, and her DVD collection includes every Demi Moore movie ever made. When you're together, you pick up on her attitude, prompting you to wonder why her mother didn't name her Always, as in Always Right.

She's noticing a few things as well, like the last time you dropped by her apartment and shared a delivery pizza with her, you used her hair as dental floss. She found out that your mother still irons your underwear and that your idea of a fun Sunday afternoon is watching bass-fishing derbies on ESPN2. She's never seen the inside of your place because "it still needs straightening up," and your idea of a Saturday night on the town is stopping at a SONIC Drive-In for a corn dog.

As Yankee catcher Yogi Berra once said, "You can observe a lot by watching," and dating partners on both sides of the table need to be observant after a relationship has started. No matter how compatible an online dating service says you are or how many interests match up perfectly like pieces in a jigsaw puzzle, your eyes need to be wide open—because if you don't like what you see or what you hear, you should be thinking exit strategy.

People come in various ways to the realization that a relationship should not continue. Maybe the phone calls and text messages have slowed to a trickle, the excuses about being busy have increased, and you're left with a sense that you're closer to the end than to the beginning of the relationship. If you're honest with yourself, you could say that she's just not that into you, to play off the title of a popular book by Greg Behrendt and Liz Tuccillo. Behrendt says, "If a sane guy really likes you, there ain't nothing that's going to get in his way."[1]

So whether she's not that into you or you realize that you don't want to spend the rest of your life watching Demi Moore movies, it's time to break off the relationship and cut your emotional losses. Breaking up correctly can be just as important as finding the right person, which is why we want to talk about how to break up in a way that honors your dating partner.

## WHEN IT'S OVER, IT'S GOT TO BE OVER

**Amy:** Let's say an online dating site declares that you're a match with someone, but after the first in-person date, you wonder if there was a computer glitch. You're as mismatched as Carmen Electra and Dennis Rodman—beauty and the beast. It's time to go your separate ways.

Unless ruthlessness is one of your character traits (and it might be if you're the Leader type), it's usually pretty tough to split up. After all, you've invested a lot of emotional energy—as well as $49.95 a month—to meet someone you're supposed to be compatible with, only to discover that it'll never work. Or maybe at one time you did think it would work, and you spread the news about the new person in your life via your IM group and Aunt Sally, the nonstop chatterbox in the family. Or maybe you've been together several years, like Jeff and I had been, and have made a huge investment of time and emotional energy.

It's our opinion that a dating relationship is always smooth and easygoing at the beginning since couples rarely disclose their faults or shortcomings. Both put their best feet forward and avoid conflict because they want the relationship to grow. Only later do faults and personality quirks surface.

If you see qualities, habits, or attitudes that give you pause, that's a warning signal that this person may not be The One. For example, if you're having major arguments or if you have broken up several times along the way, those are clear signals that you should give serious thought to ending the relationship. When red flags are sprouting like dandelions, it's definitely time to stop seeing each other.

So how do you end a relationship? Breaking off a relationship is never easy; it's been the fodder of love songs for generations…and breaking up is hard to do. Amy and I are aware that this is easier said than done, especially with some personality types. Leaders have no problem acting unilaterally to end a relationship, but Adventurers wonder if this means the end of the party. If you're the personality type that shuns confrontation or avoids intimacy, you'll have to find a way to say, "This is not going to work." Delay only makes the act of breaking up that much harder.

Which leads us to two things we need to address here:

1. What are the red flags in a relationship? How do you know it is time to end the relationship?

2. How do you end the relationship in a way that honors you and your soon-to-be ex?

## Relationship Red Flags

A good place to start is by asking yourself how you've been treated. Do you often feel degraded or unimportant? This is a red flag, and so is any hint of violence. Someone who's physically pushing you around or acting like he or she will hit you—does that bode well for a good marriage? Don't think so.

Pornography or some other kind of sex addiction is a huge red flag. I once counseled a young woman who had only one month left in her engagement. Everything was looking great: she was in love, she felt loved, but then she discovered serious amounts of porn on her fiancé's computer. He was having perverted chats with strange women and was totally addicted to the nastiest types of online porn. She wanted to know what to do, and I kindly looked at her and said, "Leave him immediately and thank God for allowing you to see this before you got married."

I'm not saying that people with pasts aren't worth marrying, because everyone has a past. But do not fool yourself into thinking that marriage will make him or her better. You want to be with someone who has overcome and triumphed from the past, not someone who is in the throes of a sickness.

You need to say no to the neurotic. Everyone has quirks, but neuroses go a bit too far. *Neurotic* is defined as "a person prone to excessive anxiety and emotional upset." If you think you're going to somehow fix this individual by your love, you're mistaken. People who have a difficult time dealing with everyday life will have an even harder time in marriage. When the anxiety of life becomes overwhelming, then depression can set in. Depression and other anxiety disorders can be treated but need to be under control before individuals afflicted with these problems are in significant relationships.

Another red flag is when your potential mate veers away from making a commitment. That's what happened to me with Jeff when he kept moving the wedding date, much like moving the goalposts just before a field-goal kicker attempts a three-pointer.

It can be difficult bringing up the subject of marriage. How long have you been together? When you're out of college, or out of graduate school, one or two years is probably a good amount of time to date, as long as you're living in the same town and see each other at least weekly. If you've been with someone for several years and you're both out of school, then you should start asking yourself why the two of you can't commit to marriage.

## Ending It Honorably

I know it can be very uncomfortable and downright painful to make someone unhappy or angry as the result of breaking up, but there are steps you can take to minimize the emotional pain. Remind yourself that it's not healthy to remain in a relationship because you are afraid to hurt someone's feelings. The pain will always be greater the longer you wait.

Be as truthful as possible about why you want to break up without assigning blame or attacking the person's character.

Break it off cleanly. Don't mouth something about remaining friends, because that could raise false hopes and prolong the inevitable, which just ends up making the pain worse. Take some time apart. After wounds heal and emotions settle, you might be able to renew a friendship, but that should not be the expectation of either of you.

**Michael:** I once dated a girl for six months when I never actually wanted to date her at all! I felt horrible every minute about the situation, but I was too nice to break up because I didn't want to hurt her feelings. What a pathetic excuse to avoid reality. Instead of saving her feelings, I made it worse because the longer we dated, the more she liked me and the less I liked her. I made everything a whole lot worse by not being honest at the very beginning. Shame on me!

**Amy:** What if you are on the receiving end of a breakup? You have every right to feel hurt and angry, but you must heal and get on with your life. Listen to the reasons behind the breakup. Does anything make sense? You deserve to know the truth, but don't expect a forum where you can debate your counterpoints. It's over. Accept your ex's feelings, even if you don't agree.

Do not, under any circumstances, attempt to force a continuation of the relationship. Let your partner go if he or she does not want to be in a relationship any longer. Remember that it takes time to heal from the wounds of a breakup, so cut yourself some slack. Do not hesitate to seek professional counseling or join a support group if the pain continues.

Get involved in activities and spend time with other people as soon as possible. Don't go running back to the computer to find your next online relationship. We suggest that you let some time pass so that you can recover from the past relationship before you pronounce yourself available again. Think in terms of weeks and months rather than days.

This is one piece of advice I heard but did not heed. Our first year of marriage would have been so much better if I had taken the time to heal from my breakup with Jeff. I was so insecure about myself. Even though I knew Michael was the best person for me, I was still hurt and angry. Had I dealt with my feelings of rejection, inadequacy, and abandonment right away, Michael and I would have had dozens and dozens fewer fights. And a better love life, as you'll read about in the next chapter.

**Think About It**

**Talk About It**

- What have you found to be the upsides and downsides of your dating experiences?
- The Bible says that it's important to "guard your heart" (Proverbs 4:23). What do you think are some ways to guard your heart while dating?
- What have you found are the more serious red flags in a dating relationship?
- Breaking up is hard to do, but why is it critical to know how to break off a relationship in a healthy and honorable way?
- What do you find most difficult about breaking up?

# 7

# If You're Having Sex, You'd Better Read This!

**M**ichael: Amy and I travel extensively and speak on many weekends at churches and conference centers. Often during our conferences, we'll ask participants to take a survey that tells us a little about who they are.

After filling out demographic information, we ask two pertinent questions that they can simply answer yes or no:

- "Are you a Christian?"
- "Did you have sex with someone other than your current spouse?"

Across the board, 80 percent of those who say they are Christians admit to having premarital sex with someone other than their current spouses. So I'm figuring there's a strong chance you've already gone all the way. That's reality, and our stance on premarital sex is this: it's not a heaven-or-hell issue, but there are consequences to sin. What you do sexually *before* you marry will definitely carry into your marriage bed.

If you are sexually active, you probably feel guilty about it and would rather keep that part of your life hidden. In counseling young couples, I've found that even though they're having sex with each other, they don't talk about what's happening. They keep having sex because they keep setting themselves up for it—by staying up late at night, being alone somewhere, making out, and revving up their engines. Sooner, rather than later, the rpm's reach redline status and something's got to blow. Afterward, they're wracked with guilt and promise each other that they must stop, and they agree they shouldn't be doing this. Yet it happens again and again.

**Amy:** The dangers of premarital sex are manifold. Everyone knows about the physical dangers of AIDS and STDs; the refrain to "protect yourself" or "wear a condom" is like cultural white noise. What you don't hear is that jumping the gun blinds you to the realities of the person you're having sex with. You're much more at risk to marry someone you shouldn't when you're having sex with him because you're not looking at him as he truly is. This is because sex does what it's supposed to do: it draws you two together, connecting you at a very deep level, even if you're sleeping with an idiot. Sorry to be so blunt, but that's how strong the bond is when you're sexually intimate with someone.

The sad mistake is that sex can blind you to your lover's problems and issues. Thoughts can rumble through your mind, such as, *I didn't want to, but now that we had sex, I obviously need to marry this person.* More often than not, that would be a tragic mistake. "The introduction of sex in the dating relationship is almost always the ushering in of the breakup of that relationship," say therapists Les and Leslie Parrott in their book *Relationships*.[1]

**Michael:** Since Amy and I know some readers of this book are virgins and others are sexually experienced, we're going to tell a few stories from those varying perspectives. You see, Amy had sex with Jeff during their relationship, and I was a virgin the day Amy and I married. As they say just before the commercial break, you'll want to stay tuned.

## A BOMBSHELL

When Amy flew back to Texas after spending five whirlwind days in Branson with me, her older sister, Suzanne, just *had* to ask her how everything went.

"Do you think you'll be seeing him again?" she asked.

"Somehow, I don't think that's going to be a problem," Amy replied.

"Why do you say that?"

"Because I'm going to marry him."

"Oh my gosh!"

The game was on for both of us. We were falling in love and felt like we were sliding down Alice in Wonderland's rabbit hole, a kaleidoscope of colors and emotions swirling in one fantastic mix. Since I couldn't wait until mid-August to see Amy again, and to be nearer to her in Texas, we decided I would fly down to Houston the following week to see her and meet her parents. It was to be my senior year at Baylor; Amy had graduated in June and was working for a political consulting firm in Houston.

On the first day of my trip, Amy planned this great date at Lake Conroe. We rented Jet Skis and had an absolute blast getting air across the wakes. (Remember, I wanted someone who wasn't fearful.) We followed it up with a romantic dinner at the La Strada restaurant. Later that evening, we found ourselves in the family room at her parents' home. We were alone, filling the air with breezy conversation, when a grim look suddenly came over Amy's face. I panicked. *Oh no,* I thought. *Here it comes. She's going to dump me.*

"There's something I *have* to tell you, that you need to know," she began.

I cringed and waited for the other shoe to drop. *She doesn't like me...there's another guy...after today she knows I'm not the one for her...*

Amy began crying, the tears slowly streaming down her face. "I... I need to let you know that I'm not a virgin," she sobbed. "So now that you know that, I can understand why you will not want to continue this relationship."

I was absolutely dumbfounded. Not because she wasn't a virgin, but because she was so sure that I would dump her once I heard this news. I remained quiet and processed what she had just said.

A brainstorm swept over me. Without saying a word, I stood up and walked to the adjacent bathroom. I found a bowl and a washcloth and filled the bowl with water. I carefully carried the bowl and placed it on the carpet next to her feet.

I began to take off her shoes. "Look, I just want you to know how much I care for you and how important you are to me," I explained. "I want you to know how unbelievable I think you are and that I would never break up with you over this."

With that, I began slowly washing her feet, a symbolic act that was first demonstrated by Christ when He washed the feet of His disciples (see John

13). I looked up at Amy while I continued to wash and massage her feet. I could see guilt written all over her face, that she believed she was less valuable as a person because she'd had sex before marriage. She knew I was a virgin; along the way in our friendship, I had made that fact known.

"Look," I said as I patted her feet dry. "I don't know of any better way to tell you this, but you are clean in my eyes, and I forgive you if that is what you need. But most importantly, I want you to know that God has already forgiven you."

**Amy:** I can't express how powerful that moment was for me. Later on, I told Michael how things transpired. Jeff and I began dating when I was a senior in high school. We kept the relationship going while he attended the University of Texas in Austin and I shook pompoms and did the bear claw at Baylor. One hundred miles separated us—not an insurmountable distance.

Over the next couple of years, things began to progress both physically and emotionally. During part of that time, he broke up with me, and I thought that happened because we didn't have that special bond of sex. So I manipulated him into a situation where we made love.

Did that rekindle our on-again, off-again relationship? Yes, for the short term. We even became engaged after that. But as several months passed, I noticed that I was so needy and he was so distant.

I thought that making love would secure his love, but it didn't. Instead of feeling secure about us, I felt extremely insecure. Not only did our relationship disintegrate, but I felt disappointed with myself. And I knew I had disappointed God.

**Michael:** Now fast-forward to my side of the story, which begins on our wedding day. I don't remember much about our wedding reception except for being pelted with rose petals—not rice, per our request—as we slipped into a white limo for the ninety-minute drive to our hotel at the Dallas/Fort Worth airport.

I was pretty excited on the drive to DFW. Something I had daydreamed about since I was a kid would soon happen. When we checked into the DFW Marriott, we were presented with the keys to the honeymoon suite on the penthouse floor.

"Ooh, look at this!" Amy said, as we walked through the well-appointed two-room suite.

"Look, Amy, we have an oversized bathtub!"

"This is fun!"

We jumped on the bed to check out the springs. "It's sturdy," I pronounced. But it was close to 7:00 p.m., and we had barely eaten all day. At the wedding reception, we'd been so busy having our pictures taken and visiting with friends and relatives that we never got a chance to pass through the buffet line. I had eaten a slice of the husband's cake (actually a brownie) during the limo ride to tide me over.

"Hey, are you hungry?" I asked my bride.

She nodded, so we ordered room service and ate in, trying to relax because we were excited about what would happen in the next hour.

Well, we had a great night together. There were lots of fireworks, and all I can tell you is, "Wow, that was worth the wait!"

But I have to be honest. Even though our wedding night deserves to be in neon lights, Amy and I experienced a really rocky first year of marriage, in part because I worried about how I measured up compared to Jeff.

**Amy:** Phew, I know this is heavy stuff. Believe me, I felt guilty because I knew my actions were not what God wanted for me. In the back of my mind, I knew that waiting for sex until marriage was the right thing, but I chose to ignore the wisdom of my parents and God.

If you can identify with me, please know there is hope, even if you're thinking, *What's the use? I can't go back and change my past.* You can change your future by confessing your sin and asking God to forgive you. When you do that, it's as though you never had sex with your partner (or partners). The Lord tells us in Isaiah 43:25 that "I—yes, I alone—will blot out your sins for my own sake and will never think of them again." Of course, God's forgiveness doesn't immediately erase the emotional consequences of your actions. So once God has forgiven you, it's important to forgive yourself and overcome the guilt and emotional baggage you've been carrying around.

It's worth it to reserve sex for marriage. You'll be protected from a host of sexually transmitted diseases, protected from the possibility of becoming a parent before you are mature enough or financially able to support and raise that child, protected from shame and the realization that you've disappointed God, and protected from making sexual comparisons when you marry.

After I broke up with Jeff, I repented for what I had done and promised God that I would not have sex again until my wedding night. It was my commitment to that goal that kept Michael and me from having sexual intercourse prior to marriage. We set good physical boundaries and kept them.

## WHAT GUYS ARE REALLY AFTER

**Michael:** Let's backtrack a bit. As you get to know and fall in love with that special person, you will feel extreme pressure to show your love in the most intimate and pleasurable way possible, and that's in bed. Let's face it: love wants to express itself in the most physical manner; for guys, the sooner the better.

From our experience, we've learned that many singles are having sex because our sex-saturated media never lets up on sending the everyone-is-having-sex-and-loving-it message. As we mentioned earlier, the popular culture says that guys and girls who meet at a crosswalk are one date away from getting it on. With sex openly discussed everywhere, just a click away on the Internet, and joked about on our entertainment shows, it's easy to have sex on the brain.

If you're still a virgin, we salute you while noting that you are a member of a minority group. Amy and I know that plenty of Christian singles are having sex these days. We know that because they *tell* us.

When you have sex before marriage, nine times out of ten the relationship cannot stand the pressure. You will end up destroying what you spent so long building. If you want your relationship to last, then the last thing you ought to do is have sex.

**Amy:** Here's what God has to say about the way we should conduct ourselves sexually:

God's will is for you to be holy, so stay away from all sexual sin.
Then each of you will control his own body and live in holiness and
honor—not in lustful passion like the pagans who do not know
God and his ways. (1 Thessalonians 4:3–5)

So put to death the sinful, earthly things lurking within you. Have
nothing to do with sexual immorality, impurity, lust, and evil

desires. Don't be greedy, for a greedy person is an idolater, worshiping the things of this world. (Colossians 3:5)

But among you there must not be even a hint of sexual immorality, or of any kind of impurity, or of greed, because these are improper for God's holy people. (Ephesians 5:3, NIV)

Did you know the word *immorality* comes from the Greek word *pornea*, which is where we get the word *pornography?* Pornea refers to any sexual indulgence outside the permanent relationship of marriage, says pastor Chip Ingram, author of *Love, Sex & Lasting Relationships.* Sex is God's gift to married couples: He designed it, He's proud of it, He wants you to do it—but also to wait until just the right time.[2]

When you indulge in sex before marriage, your motives are for yourself and not the other person. Focusing on sex makes it an idol, a replacement for God. We heard about a guy who said, "As a male, sex is what I thought about morning, noon, and night. So you would imagine that having sex would [be] the…crowning achievement in the worship of my 'god.' And yet, there was always a lack of fulfillment afterward." He added that he experienced "love hangovers" after sleeping with girls in college. "The next morning, I always felt an emptiness," he said. That's what happens when you mingle the waters of love and sex outside of marriage.[3]

It's amazing how distant I became from my family when I was sexually impure, how distant God seemed from me, and how lonely I felt. That secret world I helped create was degrading, consuming, and numbing.

**Michael:** One of the best ways to keep things in check is to be thinking long term when things get passionate. So many couples get caught up in the sexual excitement, and before they know it, clothes are flying everywhere. It's hard to back up on the freeway of sex. When you are tempted to go too far physically, think about how important sexual purity is to your future. Remember, sex is a servant of love, not the other way around. When you engage in sex before you get married, you run a very high risk of sex becoming a self-serving end.

A question we get asked a lot is, how far is too far? Please understand that Amy and I live in reality. The lines of physical contact become more and more blurred the longer you date. However, a wise couple will set limits to their expression of physical love until they get married. As a couple, take this opportunity to show some restraint. Mature love can wait. Don't degrade your first sexual expression to each other by fulfilling a release of testosterone. It is a tragedy for believers to view sex the way the world does. Some men and women view sexual interactions to be as common as shaking hands.

It wasn't too long ago that Monica Lewinsky did her thing with President Clinton in the Oval Office. That's when oral sex left the pages of the *Playboy Forum* and leaped onto the front pages of our daily newspapers. Everyone started talking about oral sex, and kids were listening, especially to what Monica and Bill were saying. The former White House intern said she and the president weren't having sex; they were just "fooling around." And President Clinton argued that their sexual encounter did not rise to the legal definition of sex. Sure, and that wasn't semen that stained Monica's famous navy blue dress, right?

Well, the only good thing to come out of that tawdry affair is that it's easier to bring up the topic of oral sex in my premarital counseling. In fact,

I like to know what I'm getting into with young couples, so I always probe into their sexual histories. That can be significant because if one or both are sexually experienced, there's usually guilt involved, and that's something you definitely want to deal with in premarital counseling.

I remember the time I was counseling Rick and Rhonda. "You don't have to answer any of these questions," I began, "but it would help me help you if I can ask you several questions about your sexual pasts. Would that be okay?"

They both nodded, so I proceeded. "Have either of you ever had sex?" I asked.

They both turned to each other and shrugged.

"No, I haven't," Rick stated.

"Me neither," said Rhonda.

"Very good. Have either of you had oral sex?"

Without batting an eye, they both said, "Sure."

Right then I knew that we had a junior version of Monica and Bill. When I prompted them for more information, their attitudes were, *It's no big deal; at least we're not having sex.*

That's the prevailing attitude these days. I heard about a young guy who lived in a single-parent home. His mother wasn't home much, so he invited guys and gals to come over to his house to drink and hang out in his Jacuzzi. A next-door neighbor overheard him saying to one of the girls, "Hey, you, come over here and give me [oral sex]," and off came his bathing suit in the Jacuzzi. It was his for the asking.

That's how casual oral sex has become these days. It's like kissing. Our stance, however, is that oral sex is something you don't want to experience because it's an intimate practice reserved for marriage. If you're having oral sex because you're trying not to have sexual intercourse, you will not make it to your wedding day without going all the way. Your body will eventually become desensitized, and you'll crave more.

That's why you should set limits early. Be thinking ahead of time so that your emotions won't run away with you in the heat of the moment. When you state your limits right up front—especially on the first date— you usually never have to make a stand again. We heard about one girl who told her date, "In case you're wondering, I have drawn my limit at my neck, so if you have any plans for dating me for any period of time, you'd better pace yourself."

You can stack the odds to maintain your boundaries by not going into her place for a last kiss or watching a video at your place when your room-mates are gone. You need accountability, so don't be afraid to ask someone else to help. We were created to be in community, so act like it! Besides, it's those little things that keep you from doing *big* things.

If kissing is your limit, you might think about taking a holiday from kissing every now and then so that smooching still feels special. Remember, sex is progressive and always wants to rush forward at the speed of light.

Whenever I do my premarital counseling, I get graphic—not in a bad way, but I get to the nitty-gritty. At the end of *More Than a Match,* I'll share some things that will help you have the best physical relationship with that special person. But until then, we're going to talk about other skills that can lead to a lasting and passionate marriage.

# Think About It

## Talk About It

- Since it's clear that God says we should have sex only in marriage, why do so many people round all the bases while still single? What's up with that?
- We feel strongly that what you do sexually before you get married affects your marriage bed. Do you agree or disagree? Why?
- What is God saying to you about your physical relationship right now? How do you feel about that?

# Conflict **Ahead**

**M**ichael: On our honeymoon, when Amy and I walked in gloomy silence to the baggage claim in San Juan, I was determined to remain as tight-lipped as possible. I was ticked off that my bride of one day hadn't told me she'd already vacationed in Puerto Rico with her former fiancé, Jeff.

For someone who had grown up with my father's *Hidden Keys of a Loving, Lasting Marriage* videos on constant loop in the background, I sure didn't have a clue how to handle conflict. What Amy had done burned me up, which fueled feelings of resentment and anger as we boarded the cruise ship *Windward*. We fought so much that I demanded we go home early, which cut short our disastrous honeymoon. Both of us emotionally limped back to Waco with our tails between our legs.

Why did we cut short a *honeymoon,* which is supposed to be the most idyllic vacation a couple can take? Who would be crazy enough to do that?

A couple in conflict.

Let me paint a complete picture: we weren't in turmoil all the time, just most of the time. Life marched on as we set up housekeeping in a small apartment not far from the Baylor campus, where I was in the midst of my senior year. Meanwhile, Amy took a job at Victoria's Secret at the local mall. I'm not making this up. (The best part of her working there was her 20 percent employee discount.)

For the first half year or so of our marriage, I couldn't cope with the fact that Amy had slept with someone else. It bugged me. Tore me up inside. Even though we were married and Amy was mine (and I was hers), all sorts of insecurities bubbled to the surface.

Suddenly, I became gripped with a desire to have her recount the more lurid details of their love affair. I wanted to know how many times they did it, when the last time was, where they were—stuff like that. My grilling didn't stop there: I asked Amy point-blank what she did with other guys.

When she replied, "Nothing," I didn't believe her. I called her a liar, which didn't exactly promote oneness in our marriage. Why did I do that? I couldn't figure myself out, so I knew I needed a good dose of therapy, which I received the following fall when we moved to Illinois and both began attending Wheaton College. Amy and I were both on track to earn postgraduate degrees in clinical psychology, and I was just a year ahead of her.

This is what I learned from meeting with a counselor during those unhappy times: the comparison thing that I was doing was more about me than about her former fiancé. I felt insecure because Amy and I had only been an item for six months or so before we got married, yet she and her former fiancé had gone out for four years before they had called it quits.

The other big thing I learned is that it wasn't too smart asking Amy for details about her past physical relationship. It didn't help. When Amy did share things about her past love life, it only made matters worse. The information made it harder for me to cope with the past. Before we married, she had shared with me in total honesty everything that I needed to know. It would have been wiser at that time to have had a third party help us deal with this issue. Sometimes your perspective on a situation needs to be broadened by someone else taking a look.

Amy and I would have probably divorced had we not been Christians and agreed that divorce was not an option for us. Thank goodness we had those things going our way. I believe that the "love is a decision" mantra that my father always preached is what got us through.

## Divorce Risk Factors

Another big thing happened when I attended a training seminar led by the premier researchers on marriage and family in the country, Scott Stanley, PhD, and Howard Markman, PhD, codirectors of the Center for Marital and Family Studies at the University of Denver. This seminar, derived from their book *Fighting for Your Marriage,* is where I learned about the four risk factors for divorce. Drs. Stanley and Markman also outlined the reasons why couples divorce, which were based on studies of 135 couples taken over a twelve-year period, couples who began the study before they were married.

After plowing through the data, Drs. Stanley and Markman were able to determine which couples were headed for divorce with up to 91 percent accuracy, based on four risk factors they developed. These risk factors were escalation, invalidation, negative interpretations, and withdrawal and avoidance.[1]

## Escalation

I'm not talking about a Cadillac SUV popular with the hip-hop crowd but about the way arguments spiral out of control to the point where the yelling can be heard in the next apartment. Partners are zinging out negative comments right and left without thinking about the impact of their words or realizing that they can't take back what they said ("Why did I ever marry you?" or "The day we divorce will be the happiest day of my life!").

## Invalidation

Dr. Stanley says that invalidation is a pattern in which the husband or wife subtly or directly puts down his or her spouse. Those who belittle their partners mutter things like, "You're an idiot. I can't believe I'm still with you." The digs are degrading and dishonoring.

Sarcasm reigns in these relationships. When a wife gets after her husband for leaving newspapers and mail strewn around the house, he'll respond with something like, "Well, sorry I'm not perfect like you." A guy who makes an innocent comment about who's coming over for a Saturday night barbecue might hear his wife say, "You're not allowed to touch the barbecue. You'd probably burn the hamburgers like you did last time."

The underlying message behind belittling comments is that the partner's feelings don't matter. I know that when I got upset with Amy during our first year of marriage, it was because I wasn't feeling validated, which led me to lash out in frustration and with hurt feelings.

**Amy:** Here's an example of a conflict that happened in our household. This particular fight occurred a number of years into our marriage. One Sunday afternoon, Michael and I were planning to have guests over for dinner and a Bible study. Michael noticed that I looked tired again. (I know, I'm always looking tired, but my excuse is that I'm the mother of three young children.) On this occasion, he told me to take a nap while he cleaned up around the house. I must have napped for about an hour. When I woke up, I looked around only to discover that the house didn't look like it had been straightened up at all. When I found Michael, he was hunched over his computer, tapping away. Oh, was I mad!

"I can't believe you're on the computer and haven't picked up the house! What did you do when I was asleep? Have you been buying stuff on the Internet again?"

Michael frowned. "I was cleaning from room to room up until five minutes ago," he said. "Then I remembered I needed to e-mail someone. What's your problem? Isn't the house clean?"

"You've got to be kidding me!" I exclaimed. "You think the house is clean! Did you not see the toys on the stairs?"

"No."

"Did you not see the dishes in the sink?"

"No."

"Can't you see the floor needs to be swept?"

"I did that!"

I glanced at the hardwood floors. If he had swept them, he sure hadn't done a good job. I threw up my hands in frustration.

That little episode didn't end well, and you can see how invalidating I was. Michael, in what I thought was a futile attempt, was trying to help.

My attitude discounted everything he did. It took me a long time to understand that Michael doesn't see clutter the way I do. That afternoon, I devalued his efforts when I didn't acknowledge what he had done or tried to do.

**Michael:** We're doing better in this area, I'm happy to report.

## Negative Interpretations

**Michael:** Dr. Stanley said that negative interpretations occur when one partner consistently believes that the motives of the other are more negative than is really the case. In other words, your partner can't do anything right.

I love telling the following joke to illustrate how this looks. There was a husband and wife who were constantly crabbing at each other because he was coming home later than expected after getting off work. The husband wanted to shrug it off, but his wife wouldn't let him off the hook. After several times of this happening, he felt bad and wanted to make things right, so after leaving work a little early, he swung by a supermarket and picked up some flowers and a card to make amends.

"Honey, I'm home!" he announced as he swept past the front door shortly after 5:00 p.m.

His wife eyed the handsome bouquet of red roses and broke down weeping, brushing back tears.

This was obviously not the joyful response he was hoping for. "Honey, what's wrong?" he asked.

"You won't believe the day I've had," she said as she smeared the mascara under a pair of tired eyes. "The kids have been horrible, the house is a mess, and now my husband comes home drunk."

That is a negative interpretation, because she never imagined that her husband would come home when he said he would or bring her flowers for no other reason than out of the goodness of his heart.

## Withdrawal and Avoidance

This was the place I scampered to when conflict reared its ugly head between Amy and me. When I was unhappy with her or perceived a slight, I wouldn't address what happened or initiate any discussion. That inappropriate response ensured that the pain would never end. I was unwilling to get into or stay in a discussion that could be threatening to me. I shut down because that's where I felt emotionally safe.

## DEALING WITH THE RISK FACTORS

Each of the four risk factors—escalation, invalidation, negative interpretations, and withdrawal and avoidance—can erect formidable communication barriers in a relationship. Drs. Stanley and Markman's research over the years shows that couples who want good relationships need to eliminate these risk factors early and as often as they sneak back in, or else the negative factors will take their relationships down a track where the final stop is named Splitsville.

Young couples, even those validated for their compatibility by sites like eHarmony.com, need to recognize these four risk factors as their relationships begin to grow.

**Amy:** If any of these four risk factors creep up during conflict, you may as well erect a road sign that says Trouble Ahead. Michael and I batted a perfect four for four on our honeymoon. Our disagreements quickly escalated, so we stopped validating each other, which caused us to believe negative things about each other, which led to his withdrawal and silent treatment.

These days, we are much more aware of when escalation is happening, which is something we want to nip in the bud before the situation ends up with one or both of us sulking. We had to learn to put boundaries on our discussions and try to follow something that Michael's father calls LUV Talk: Listen, Understand, and Validate.[2]

One aspect of LUV Talk is that you're not allowed to argue during fun time—such as dates, honeymoon, and vacations. If we had followed that rule in the Caribbean, we never would have argued about silly stuff. Today, we know better. Whenever we go on a date or out to dinner or leave for a long weekend, that time is safe. We won't argue, no matter what direction the conversation veers. We will not fight. If it's a big enough issue, we'll say, "Let's not get into it now, but let's resolve this when we get home."

It took Michael and me more than a few years to reach that point, so don't think you'll get there overnight. The fact of the matter is that men and women say stupid things because they don't realize their words can hurt so much. For that reason, we made up a list of statements that we will never say to each other, statements like "I want a divorce" or "I hate you."

One time Michael said in the heat of an argument, "You're being ___." He used a word that rhymes with itchy. Boy, did I give him flak for that, and he deserved it. He had stepped over the line, a line that we don't want you to step over in your relationship.

## LOOKING AHEAD

**Michael:** After experiencing marital turmoil firsthand and in talking with couples in my counseling practice, I can reliably state that the first year of marriage is often the toughest. Reality crashes on the shore like a tsunami because two people of different genders, different temperaments, and (usually) different personalities are told to become one. Even perfect-match couples soon find that a perfect match doesn't mean perfect agreement.

Looking ahead, we see several hot-button issues that couples need to discuss before they get married. (Keep in mind that these are items that a good premarital counselor will zero in on.) You may be discovering that you're not as compatible as you thought, but don't give up. With a third party guiding the discussion, you must talk about the big items: in-laws, parenting styles, if and when you'll have children, finances, sex, communication, careers, housework, recreation, and religion. Those are the biggies. If you skirt around those, you'll get stuck in hip-deep mud.

**Amy:** Don't think, *Well, we'll deal with that when we get married.* Where would you be if after the wedding your husband says, "I want to have five kids," but you say, "We won't ever have children. I hate children. I was an only child, and that's the way I feel." Bam! You have a major problem on your hands.

I remember the time I counseled an engaged couple that had an issue with male and female roles. He was saying that the man rules and is the final authority on everything, while she was saying that she deserved an equal say in important matters. After I explained that they needed to operate as a team and that couples should make decisions through a consensus-building grid, I saw his heart and demeanor soften. Progress had been made for a couple about to embark on the biggest adventure of their lives. Here are some other questions that premarital couples need to tackle.

**Who's going to do the household chores?** Answer: both of you, because this goes back to what your primary attitude about marriage should be, which is, *How can I serve my spouse?* Guys, if you're thinking about lollygagging with the remote or huddling with your computer to surf the Net after dinner, you're thinking of yourself first. Helping out in the kitchen—before, during, and after dinner—is a way you can serve your wife. Take the lead during kitchen cleanup.

The domestic sciences, as we call them, are roundly discussed in our premarital counseling with couples. How can you help each other out? How difficult is it to run a vacuum over a rug or mop a kitchen floor? How can a guy shed the attitude that cleaning up around the house is "women's work"?

**Michael:** It helps to know your strengths and weaknesses regarding housework. For instance, I'm horrible at putting folded laundry away. I can take a neatly folded stack of shirts and stuff them into a drawer in a way that would give Martha Stewart the vapors. Amy and I have learned that it's better for our marriage if she puts the folded laundry away because she's much neater than me.

But that doesn't mean I abdicate my role as a helpmate. I've found out that I'm pretty good at taking clothes out of the dryer and folding them nicely; I just can't put them away neatly. I've also discovered that I'm even better at folding laundry when I watch ESPN's SportsCenter. It's called redeeming the time.

Guys, if you want something done special, like the way your jockstraps are ironed, then iron them yourself. I've become quite handy with the iron, so much so that even my father and my brother, Greg, will ask me to run an iron over their dress shirts when we're out on a speaking tour together. This doesn't actually do anything for my masculinity, but I'm okay with that.

**How many cooks in the kitchen?** Formerly thought to be the province of women, the kitchen is an equal opportunity employer. Cooking (and the subsequent cleanup) can be done by men, the last time I checked. Aren't many great chefs male?

**Amy:** My view on the art of cooking boils down to one sentence: if you can read, you can cook. There are so many cookbooks and recipes floating around the Internet that the "I can't cook" excuse cannot be accepted. Michael is mean on the grill. He bought a Big Green Egg (a smoker/barbecue grill based on the ancient Asian Kamado). Using it has helped Michael master the art of cooking steaks, shrimp, burgers, chicken, and fish to perfection. We have a lot of fun when he grills and I cook the sides.

If your wife-to-be is more gifted in the kitchen than you are, you can become the assistant chef, the person chopping up the onion or preparing the salad or scrubbing some pots and pans. The old adage "Many hands make light work" certainly applies in the kitchen.

**Michael:** Let us make another point about cooking: in the quest to make ends meet as a young couple, look at your kitchen as a profit center. Yes, the more you eat home-cooked meals, the more money you will save. And in these days of expanding waistlines, you can save calories by carefully choosing your recipes.

**Who's going to do the finances in the family?** The decision of who's watching the till should be based on personality and ability, not gender. In our household, Amy does our finances. That's a better fit for us; I am not detail-oriented, and I'm prone to forgetting things—like bringing my wallet to the restaurant, remember? The one time I was put in charge of paying the bills, I got us so messed up with the electric company that they nearly turned out the lights on us.

Amy has the responsibility of paying the bills and tracking the income and outgo. She established our budget, and in our first couple of years we agreed to use the envelope system popularized by Christian financial counselor Larry Burkett. For instance, each month we would put fifty dollars in an envelope for gas (yeah right, those were the good ol' days!), a hundred and twenty dollars into an envelope marked entertainment, and so forth, including an envelope containing our tithe to God's work. The hundred-and-twenty-dollar entertainment envelope is what we earmarked to spend on eating out, going to a movie, or seeing a show. When the cash ran out, we didn't go out until the new month arrived. It was that simple, and the envelope system curbed our spending at a time when things were financially tight because of college bills.

**Amy:** We highly recommend that young couples employ the envelope system and *not* use credit cards to buy stuff and pay bills. I don't care how many airline miles you pass up, credit card usage is a surefire way to spend above your means. Christian financial counselor Ron Blue states that people have a tendency to spend 34 percent more when they reach into their wallets for a credit card instead of cash or a checkbook.[3]

Listen, we have nothing against credit cards. Life would be pretty inconvenient without plastic. Credit cards open up the universe of eBay.com and other Internet shopping sites, and you can't find your match on eHarmony.com without one. They're great for emergencies. And you don't have to worry about carrying around cash.

The problem with credit cards, however, is that you *will* spend more if you're purchasing something with a credit card. There's something about reaching into your front pocket, untangling a wad of cash, counting out your fives and ones, and *handing over* your money that acts like a monitor on overspending.

On the other hand, it's easy—way too easy—to hand over your credit card, let the cashier swipe it through a reader, and sign on the dotted line. The transaction takes a matter of seconds and then the charge is in the books.

If you can wean yourself off credit cards and pay by cash, check, or debit card (which automatically deducts the amount from your checking account), you'll save yourself tons of grief—and perhaps your marriage, since financial pressures have sunk many marriages over the years. Did you know that spending money you haven't earned is like using up years you haven't lived? Did you know that the average American family owes ninety-two hundred dollars in credit card debt, according to CardWeb.com?[4] Out-of-control credit debt will mortgage your future and stop you from purchasing your first home for *years.*

We have friends who asked for a five-thousand-dollar limit on their credit card, and when they received it, they went out and purchased a home entertainment system. After making the minimum payments for the first year, they soon realized that the 19 percent interest rate was killing them.

Our friends were among the unsuspecting millions of Americans who barely noticed that someone had pulled a warm, soothing, wool blanket over their eyes. The power of advertising convinced them that their monthly credit card statement didn't have to be paid back in full each month. Instead, they could pay the minimum amount, which the credit card company conveniently printed in a box right next to the total balance figure. Such a trifling amount.

But debt is so expensive. Maybe five thousand dollars for a home entertainment system looked manageable to our friends, but after making minimum payments and letting that 19 percent interest rate stir the pot for a year or two, they understood that they had made a horrible mistake. Scripture is fairly blunt when describing those who borrow on credit: "Just as the rich rule the poor, so the borrower is servant to the lender" (Proverbs 22:7).

This verse doesn't mean you should never borrow money. It's just a friendly warning from the Lord that you should not take a loan without carefully examining your ability to pay it back.

**How often are you going to eat out?** According to the National Restaurant Association, the average American eats food prepared in a commercial setting one out of every five meals, or 4.2 meals per week.[5] If you figure that you spend an average of $10 per meal (I'm trying to balance the difference between fast-food and sit-down restaurants), for the two of you that's $84 a week or $336 a month.

Trimming restaurant meals, takeout food, and fast-food trips is the fastest way to save a few hundred dollars each month, money you'll need to furnish a new place or begin saving for a down payment on a house. The fact remains that eating out is expensive these days, and it costs more than we often realize.

**Will the wife work outside the home? Michael:** This is usually a question that couples do not talk about until the children arrive, but it's an important one that needs to be addressed much earlier. If Amy and I had gone through comprehensive premarital counseling, I would have learned that she was not cut out to be a stay-at-home mom who baked Toll House cookies every afternoon. That's not how she is wired. She wanted a career, but one with flexible hours so that she could be with the kids during the day and not have them put into day care.

That's exactly what happened in our household. She received her master's degree in clinical psychology and began counseling couples at night when I could be home with the children. That works for me because I hate working at night. Working two or three nights a week makes her happy, and when Mom is happy, everyone is happy.

## What a Concept

**Michael:** These are just a handful of the hot-button issues that will crop up during your first year of marriage. We can think of a bunch more—how you will handle conflict, how you will you spend the holidays (with your family or your spouse's family or starting your own traditions?), how you will decorate the home, where you will take your vacations, how often you will socialize with your friends and your spouse's friends, how often you will see the in-laws, and whether you will make an out-of-town move to advance a career.

You'll have to talk about it, which is polite shorthand for the effort of working through those issues. Communication must be two-way, even if that goes against your personality type. Guys, especially, must look for ways they can serve their wives, such as being good listeners. Looking for ways to serve each other is the concept of mutual submission.

We sometimes get asked about the husband being the head of the family and what that means. We joke that a scene from the hit movie *My Big Fat Greek Wedding* says it all.

In this scene, the wise mother of the bride is talking to her daughter about how marriage will be. Keep in mind that the mother grew up in the old country, while the daughter was born in the Chicago area.

"The man might be the head of the family," said the mother, "but the woman is the neck, and she can make the head turn any way she wants!"

Don't forget that, guys!

## Think About It

## Talk About It

- Based on any conflicts you have had in more serious relationships, which of these divorce risk factors do *you* struggle with most?
    Escalation
    Invalidation
    Negative Interpretations
    Withdrawal and Avoidance
- As you prepare for marriage, what might you do to reduce the impact of the divorce risk factors that you struggle with?
- If you are in a serious relationship now, what are the hot-button issues that you and your potential spouse need to resolve before you decide to marry?

# Look for **the Easy Button**

**M**ichael: I'm the type of person who watches the Super Bowl for the game *and* the commercials. I love hearing about new products making a buzz. My impulsive personality is tailor-made for companies enticing me to swipe my credit card and walk away with their newest gadgets, and it certainly doesn't help my cause that I'm an early adopter who loves trying out the hottest technology. For example, I bought one of the first iPods when they came out back in 2001, long before the white-cased MP3 player became the coolest thing on the planet to own. I've purchased two more iPods since then because Apple added more storage and more features, like viewing digital pictures.

This attitude about the power of technology probably explains why a certain commercial caught my eye in 2006. I'm talking about the Easy

Button campaign from Staples, the office products retailer, showcasing how easy it can be to get organized. For instance, in one of the commercials, Santa Claus was shown pushing a red Easy Button to order digital cameras from a Staples store, rather than asking his elves to magically turn a wooden camera into one that takes megapixel photos.

In the Staples land of make-believe, all people have to do is press an Easy Button, and they hear a friendly voice say, "That was easy." To hype the promotional campaign, Staples outlets from Portland, Maine, to Portland, Oregon, were stocked with Easy Buttons that sold for five bucks. (Proceeds were donated to the Boys and Girls Clubs of America.)

There have been times during counseling sessions with bickering couples that I've wished that I had purchased an Easy Button and set it out for them to push. Unfortunately, resolving conflict is never as simple as punching a red button, although some couples have to be convinced otherwise. I remember teaching a marriage seminar one weekend when a couple approached me during a break. After introducing himself, the guy said, "In thirty seconds or less, I want you to fix our marriage."

I stifled a laugh because the request was so preposterous. "Can I ask why?" I inquired.

"Because we're in total crisis," he replied. "That's why we came to your marriage seminar this weekend. My wife and I have been talking about divorce."

I looked to his wife, who timidly nodded in agreement.

"How long have you been married?" I asked.

"Fifteen years," she replied.

"How long have things been stressed out?"

"About eight years."

"In other words, it took you seven or eight years to get into this, but you expect me to fix everything in thirty seconds."

I felt for the couple since what they asked was impossible, but I did leave them with this idea: the quickest way to make an instant, powerful, dramatic change in a relationship, whether you've been married fifteen years or just met online, is by changing yourself. Becoming a better friend, a better listener, and a more caring and attentive person means you're taking responsibility for yourself, your actions, and how you treat that special person in your life. A person who can say to the other, "We may not be getting along very well, but that's not going to dictate how I'll treat you," gives the relationship hope for the future.

**Amy:** I agree with Michael that taking personal responsibility for who you are, what you say, and how you act will make or break any relationship. Michael and I have had to learn this aspect of personal responsibility, and I can assure you that this concept changed and deepened my relationship with him. When you're stressed out or when things aren't going well, instead of trying to fix the problem, just ask the question, what do you need right now?

Asking that is like pushing the Easy Button. What that question says to your husband or wife is, *I'm here for you, I'm not going away, so what can I do for you?* You allow your spouse to be who he or she is in that moment, and giving permission like that will draw you closer together.

Personal responsibility means that the initiative to do something positive in the relationship camps on your shoulders. You can't wait for your special person to be doing things right in order to treat him or her well. It's not "I'll scratch your back if you scratch mine." If your love has a sore back and needs a rubdown, then knead those muscles.

One of the biggest mistakes married couples make is that when the husband comes home from work and sees that his spouse looks tired, he immediately flies into action, saying, "Let me do this! Let me do that!" More often than not, that's not what the wife needs at that moment. She needs her husband to listen to how her day went, understand everything she put up with, and validate her feelings of being physically tired and emotionally exhausted—the concept of LUV Talk that we introduced in the last chapter. A better way to start would be for the husband to say, "Honey, you look tired and exhausted. Is there anything I can do for you right now?"

You can't *assume* what you should do. I'll never forget the time Michael and I moved from Chicago to Branson because we thought it would be a good idea to live close to Michael's parents. As soon as the moving truck pulled into the driveway of our new home, Michael decided the best way he could help me would be to leave me with all the furniture and boxes while he took the kids on errands and to places like the park.

**Michael:** In my head, I honestly thought I would be helping out Amy by leaving her home alone with the moving boxes. It seemed like I always messed things up when it came to packing and unpacking because I'm so disorganized and undetailed.

She didn't say much after I took the kids to the movies and for a Happy Meal on the first day. And she was quiet when I took the kids to the movies and for Happy Meals on the second day. (In case you're wondering, yes, she should have expressed her displeasure.)

She'd finally had enough by the time the third day of unpacking boxes rolled around and I was out with the kids. She called me that afternoon and said, "Where are you?"

"I'm at McDonald's," I replied, as I watched the kids going bonkers in a play area filled with plastic balls.

"Why have you abandoned me? You're making me do all the work!"

Amy was weeping, and rightly so. Unpacking those boxes was too much to ask of one person, and even if I wasn't the most detailed person in the world, I could have done *something*. Just as James 1:19 says believers should be quick to listen, I should have been listening—or looking—for clues that being gone with the kids while Amy unpacked wasn't a good idea. I learned from that mistake, and believe me, it wasn't the first—or the last—time I blew it around the house.

Recently Amy woke me up out of a deep sleep, and I'm not the easiest guy to wake up in the middle of the night, especially at 1:00 a.m. when I've been asleep for three hours.

"Get up, now! We need to talk!" she exclaimed as she shook me awake.

My first reaction, after shaking off the effects of slumber, was to think, *What have I done?* I must have really messed up something to warrant a middle-of-the-night intrusion of my sleep.

"I need to talk to you," she said. "I was on the phone with Jessica"—someone Amy had been counseling—"when she hung up on me. I can't believe how rude she was. Couldn't she see that her life was a mess and that I was just trying to help?"

**Amy:** I didn't want to call Jessica back and bawl her out, but I needed to vent. I needed someone to talk to about it.

**Michael:** I looked at Amy. For once, I said the right thing: "Oh, that's a horrible thing to have happen. What can I do right now to help you?"

Just saying that really helped her to relax. She didn't need my help; she needed someone to talk to about Jessica. As Amy got everything off her chest, I realized that (a) she was blowing off steam, and (b) she wanted me to be supportive and encouraging, not necessarily to solve her problem. So I sat there in bed, letting her vent to her heart's content while she processed her conversation. Amy was taking personal responsibility for what had happened and not blaming me for Jessica's hanging up on her.

As you develop a relationship with a potential mate or even move toward marriage, the idea of taking personal responsibility for the way you act and the way you talk will rise in importance. In a nutshell, personal responsibility says, "I have control over my own thoughts, feelings, and actions."

**Amy:** What I told Jessica in counseling was that her boyfriend didn't make her mad; she chose to be mad. No matter how angry or upset she felt about her boyfriend, she would have to take responsibility for the way she responded to him.

Well, she didn't want to hear that. She was stuck on playing the blame game, which says to the other person, "I'm upset and hurt because of your behavior, so I'm not going to feel better until you change." That's a disastrous attitude to take, because what it does is turn you into a victim. Michael and I are well aware that victimhood is a favored cop-out in some quarters. In other words, victims blame others, not themselves, for the way life is turning out.

That's not the way to go. You are basically giving up all your power to someone else when you give in to victimhood, whereas personal responsibility says, "The buck stops with me. I have no one to blame but myself."

**Michael:** In the past, whenever I did something wrong or said something stupid in front of Amy, I tried to use my ADHD or impulsivity as an excuse not to take personal responsibility for my actions. For instance, at the beginning of this chapter I told you that I'm an early adopter, someone who just has to have the latest technology in the palm of my hand or at the touch of a button or keyboard.

Well, during the early years of the cell-phone boom, telecommunications companies would offer a free cell phone just for signing up. Every time a new cell phone hit the market, one with a few more bells and whistles than the one in my pants pocket, I would scribble my name on a contract for a new phone.

I was too impulsive to read the fine print or even ask what I was signing, but if I had, I would have learned that I was on the hook to continue with that company's cell phone service for at least one year. Canceling my old cell phone always triggered early cancellation fees of hundreds of dollars. In a period of four months, I must have tried out six new carriers—and signed six different contracts. That turned out to be a problem, and it bothered Amy, who paid the bills and saw how costly my cell phone addiction had become. If there was a twelve-step program, I'm sure Amy would have enrolled me. (I could see myself standing up in a circle of other addicts and saying, "Hi, my name is Michael, and I have cell-phone addiction.")

We finally came up with an agreement that I would not be allowed to buy a new cell phone without the express written consent of Amy Johnston Smalley. For about a year, everything went fine. On one fateful Sunday afternoon, however, we got back from church, and I saw that Amy looked tired, the kids looked tired—everyone needed some rest. So, burnishing my credentials to win a Dad of the Year award, I said to Amy, "Hey, why don't you take a nap? I'll put the kids down and do the grocery shopping for the week."

"That would be awesome," Amy replied with a wide grin.

A half hour later at the grocery store, I was minding my own business, pushing a cart down one of the aisles, when I heard a whisper in my head that could have been Satan himself.

"Psst, buddy, have your seen our new cell phone?"

The voice came from behind my peripheral vision. I stopped in mid-step. *Don't turn around,* I thought. *Don't get hooked, just keep going.* I felt a lot like Lot's wife in Genesis—that if I turned around and looked, I would be turned into a pillar of salt.

"This is the latest cell phone from AT&T, the leader in cell phone technology," I heard the voice say.

I swiveled my head, and I saw a nerdy salesman standing behind a display table, holding up a glistening example of cutting-edge technology. Then I uttered the words that sealed my fate: "I didn't know AT&T was in Branson."

The next thing I knew, I was exiting the supermarket with a cart full of groceries and a new cell phone with a signed contract. I was feeling pretty good about myself when a dark cloud appeared on the horizon: *I could potentially get into a lot of trouble over this. After all, I had agreed to clear all cell phone purchases with Amy.*

I knew what to do: come up with a cute line or funny story so Amy wouldn't get upset. *Yeah, that's the ticket.* When I got home, I put away all the groceries and tiptoed into the living room, where my lovely wife was dozing on the couch. I tapped her on the shoulder, which was my first mistake since you never wake a sleeping mom on a Sunday afternoon. A second tap caused her to open her eyes.

"Hey, you're back," she said in a sleepy stupor, but her smile said she was genuinely glad to see me.

Since my stock was so high, I figured this was my best chance. In my best Austin Powers impression, I said in a flirtatious manner, "Yeah, baby, and would you like my number?"

*Man, was that stupid.*

Amy stopped smiling. "I already have your cell phone number. Why would I need it?"

Like Wile E. Coyote, who looks to the camera just before he falls a thousand feet to the desert floor, I thought, *This is really going to go really bad.*

"Well, I have a new *num-ber,*" I sang out in a falsetto voice.

"You *what?*"

I showed her the phone, and the gauntlet was down. She immediately began escalating and getting on my case.

"This is ridiculous. You promised me that you wouldn't get a new cell phone. This is so irresponsible!"

My response was purely defensive. I could see rationally that Amy was not taking personal responsibility, because she was allowing *my* behavior to dictate how she treated me, which is not what you're supposed to do. Instead of taking the high road, though, and exercising some personal responsibility on my part, I started wagging my index finger at her. "Hey, don't talk to me like that," I declared in a huffy tone of voice.

"I will if I feel like it!"

Ooh…so I pulled out the dumbest line in history, a line that men throughout the ages have employed at one time or another with their wives. (Usually, a man will only make this mistake once!)

Here's what I said: "Hey, I'm the one who works around here, so don't tell me how to spend *my* money."

Instead of causing Amy to bow and scrape and say, "Yes, your Lordship," she went ballistic and postal, and she escalated the discussion to a point where she was totally out of control. She closed the small distance between us and jabbed her finger at me in a very aggressive way, as she breathed fire and screamed at me for how irresponsible I was.

Just then our oldest child, Cole, age five at the time, had woken up and started down the staircase. I looked up from the living room and thought, *This is not real cool.* For one reason or another, I didn't want to destroy my son's heroic image of his dad quite yet. So I looked at Amy and gave her a cutoff signal, a finger to the lips, a nonverbal gesture for her to back off.

Amy looked at Cole, looked back at me, and then launched a nuke missile my way, which assured our mutual destruction. "I *want* our son to hear how irresponsible his father is!" she huffed and puffed.

Let's just such say that with that, she touched something primal. I don't normally escalate, I don't normally get angry, and I don't normally freak out, but I couldn't let that slide.

**Amy:** It was one of those moments where I wished I could retrieve a launched missile. I knew I had crossed the line because I saw it in his eyes. I took off for the master bedroom.

**Michael:** I chased her through the living room, into our bedroom, past our bathroom, and into a small closet. Let me paint a complete picture for you of how ridiculous it was: here we had two marriage and family therapists chasing each other through their house, yelling and screaming.

**Amy:** When Michael caught up with me, he ordered me to sit down. "I can't!" I screamed. "I'm in a closet!"

**Michael:** She's such a little thing, but, boy, she just doesn't back down. We're talking about a very small closet. There was just room enough in there for us to stand nose to nose. I was as livid as ever and trying to reestablish male dominance, saying in so many words that I was the big guy here, you can't defeat me, I'm going to win this argument. I was pointing my finger at her and telling her how awful she was, just blasting her with anything I could come up with.

Her response was, *"Don't point your finger at me!"*

I couldn't seem to regain control of that argument. I was losing, and I knew it. I had to come up with something to counter her last demand, something that would show her how powerful and awe-inspiring her husband was, something that would put her back in her place.

Two options came to mind. The first thought, which would have landed me in prison for twenty years, involved a hanger and some shoestring. Well, I didn't want to spend any time in prison.

I settled on my second option, and remember, this option was to regain the power and win our argument. I reared back and roared, "You don't want me to point? You haven't seen anything yet!"

I proceeded to point at her with a machine-gun action. I was pointing index fingers from *both* hands as fast as I could.

It was the stupidest thing you can imagine. I was totally out of control, and the worst part was Amy's response. She laughed. She laughed at my masculine prowess!

Then she finished me off. "Oh, you're being serious?" she cackled. Hearing *that* sent me over the edge. I just blacked out with rage.

The story ends with her sneaking out of the closet, leaving me completely humiliated because I had done that totally idiotic pointing thing. Standing outside our bathroom was Cole, who had tears pooling in his eyes. He had never seen Mommy and Daddy in a knockdown, drag-out fight like that.

**Amy:** When I saw Cole, a splash of consciousness came over me. I knew I had gotten out of line. I asked him to follow me, and I sat him on the couch beside our bed. I told him, "I should not have said those things about your dad. I should not have yelled at him. Will you please forgive me for fighting with Daddy in front of you? I love Daddy, and I'm sorry my actions didn't show that today."

**Michael:** Just hearing her take responsibility and not blame me melted my heart—and totally changed my perception of how things transpired. Now I felt like a heel for my lack of personal responsibility—and totally convicted.

**Amy:** It was hard for me to take personal responsibility because what Michael did was wrong. But when I started to escalate, that's when I became just as wrong as he was.

**Michael:** That's the point. There are no excuses to treat people poorly, especially those you are getting to know in a relationship or have fallen in love with. I've found that when I'm nice to Amy in the little day-to-day things— listening well, communicating that I've heard her—then I'm able to validate her. I practice LUV Talk: Listening, Understanding, and Validating.

One of the best ways to live out LUV Talk is to use something we call drive-through communication, the same type of communication that you use when you swing into a fast-food drive-through lane. It's a method of back-and-forth speaking that was introduced by Drs. Howard Markman, Scott Stanley, and Susan L. Blumberg in their book *Fighting for Your Marriage*.[1] They called it the "speaker/listener technique," which my father adapted by using a McDonald's drive-through as a metaphor for what should happen in good communication. He patterned this type of drive-through conversation after how fast-food workers are trained to repeat customer orders so that no mistakes are made in completing the orders.

Here's how it works. You drive up to a McDonald's restaurant and roll down your window. You hear a voice saying, "May I take your order, please?"

You're hungry, so you rattle off, "I would like two Big Macs, fries, and a Diet Coke."

The employee rattles off, "That's two Big Macs, fries, and a Diet Coke?"

But imagine if the pimple-faced high school employee sticks his head out the window and starts looking you over, so much so that you think there is something truly wrong—you check the mirror to make sure your nose is clean. You smile: no, nothing between your teeth. And then that employee says, "Hey, I was looking at you, and I'm sorry, but you really fill up the whole front seat of your car. I think you need a McSalad instead of the Big Mac."

What would you do? You might make that drive-through lane a drive-through building with your car. How rude! Would you ever go back to that McDonalds? Would you say you might divorce yourself from all such transactions? Ah, now you're getting the point. That is you and that is me when we try to change our spouses or friends by telling them how to feel or what we think they should need.

**Amy:** That's why the employee repeats what the customer says, because he wants to be sure he understands what was communicated to him. If the employee got the order wrong, this gives the customer another chance to articulate his wishes in a different way. In LUV Talk rules, the "customer" uses "I" statements ("I would like…"), shares only feelings and needs, and keeps his comments short. The "employee" listens with ears, body, and heart, shows understanding by repeating what was heard, and validates what the customer has said.

The drive-through method of communication is a great way for cou-ples to practice their basic interaction skills. In our seminars, we recom-mend that couples take turns: one is the employee, the other is the customer. It's the employee's job to listen, try to understand, and validate what the customer said—and iron out any details to the customer's satis-faction, because when couples argue, many times they focus on the details.

She says, "You told me you'd be back by five o'clock!"

He says, "You also said we didn't have to be at the Fernwoods' barbe-cue until seven!"

That is not getting to the heart of the issue, which, in this case, may have nothing to do with him stepping through the front door at 6:00 p.m. and everything to do with him not calling to say that he *would* be late.

So instead of getting into a monologue, the guy should pretend he's wearing a paper hat and taking orders at a drive-through window. He should repeat back what she said to show that he understood and to vali-date her feelings, which meets her at the same emotional level. On her side, she should communicate her needs or feelings by saying something like, "When you were late, I felt rushed, and I don't like to be in a rush before I go out at night."

Here's what he should say as he repeats what he heard her saying: "You just said that you don't like to feel rushed before we go out to a dinner party. I'm glad you said that. Next time, I'll make sure I'm a little early so that you don't feel rushed."

That is an example of taking personal responsibility, which is the point of this chapter. Taking personal responsibility means avoiding excuses, vali-dating what you hear, and keeping your phrases short and concise. It's def-initely not using the word *you* in an accusatory manner, such as, "You're always in the bathroom when I arrive to pick you up, so I end up waiting for you anyway."

**Michael:** I admit that that sounds like something I would say, but Amy and I have gotten better at this. Remember, I'm famous for leaving dirty clothes on the floor, and Amy found that calling me irresponsible wasn't too effective. But when she said my clothes on the floor left her feeling frustrated because she liked the house to be picked up, what could I say? Of course I felt like a schlep. We had a breakthrough when I said, "So you're trying to tell me that it really frustrates you when I leave my clothes on the floor."

"Yes, that's why I'm trying to say," Amy nodded.

Bingo—drive-through communication. So I reminded myself not to leave my clothes on the floor...so often.

Since women are more verbal, it's important for a guy to make sure to reverse roles and share *his* feelings.

For instance, let's say a dating couple is engaged to be married. She says, "I think I'm getting overwhelmed with the amount of things I'm getting asked to do before the big day."

Her fiancé should not evaluate or criticize that. He shouldn't say, "Give me a break," or "That's so ridiculous."

It is what it is. If she feels it, she feels it. It's the fiancé's job to say, "Wow, it sounds like you're feeling overwhelmed with everything that's going on right now."

He may be feeling the same thing, and there will be a chance for him to say that. But for now, she's looking for her feelings to be validated.

Early in their relationships, couples will many times try to validate their feelings, opinions, or perceptions at the same time. They resemble attorneys on different sides of the courtroom, eager to score legal points but not real eager to concede ground.

Acting like opposing attorneys doesn't lead to intimacy. If you want to have a great relationship, you'll want to be thinking about meeting each other's needs and not about winning an argument. By taking your time and trying to understand the other person—and validating his or her perceptions—you will be validating that special person for who he or she is. You'll be saying, "You're okay for feeling this way, and I'm fine with that."

Another great way to defuse conflict is to think of win-win solutions. The whole concept of the win-win is that there is no such thing as a win-lose scenario. I will ask a couple, "Do you feel like you're on the same team or opposite teams?"

"Well, of course we're on the same team," a couple will say. If they believe that, they can never have a lose-lose. Win-lose scenarios sometimes come about when some man completely misunderstands the husband's role revealed in the Bible and thinks he's the ultimate decision maker. What he will often do is bulldoze over the line. For instance, let's say the family lives in Houston and he gets offered a new job in Orlando. He comes home with the news and announces, "We're moving."

"Wait a minute," the wife says. "I don't think that's a good idea."

"Well, I'm sorry. I hear what you're saying, but ultimately, this is my decision and we're moving."

A man *should not* do that. That is not biblical or healthy, and if he takes that attitude, disaster looms. A husband and wife are to become one. While Ephesians 5:22 instructs wives to submit to their husbands, the verse before very clearly says, "Submit to one another." That passage also talks about how men should love their wives as Christ loved the church. Well, how did

Christ love the church? Answer: He laid down His life because it wasn't about His agenda but about serving people unconditionally.

In that sense, if you're going to call yourself a Christian, that means being Christlike. Well, what was Christ like? Was He a domineering, pushy kind of guy who didn't validate people? No. He was very loving and came as a lamb. So if you get a new job and your wife is totally against it, your job is to lay down your life and figure out a win-win solution for both of you. You don't have permission to say, "Thanks for your opinion, but too bad."

**Amy:** And ladies, this is not the time to cop out if you don't feel like it's the best decision, muttering something like, "Oh, he's the head of the household, so whatever he says…" If something is unsettling you in your heart, spirit, or intuition, you should stay in neutral until you both feel like there's a win-win decision.

That's what Michael and I did when we began discussing a move from Branson to the Houston area a couple of years ago. When Michael and I first began talking about the possibility, he thought I would want to start packing that night because my parents live on the outskirts of Houston and moving would put me closer to my family. But something in my heart didn't feel right about moving.

**Michael:** Knowing that a major decision like that had to be a win-win for the both of us, I wasn't about to start bulldozing her and pressuring her to move, even though I felt it was the right thing to do as well as time to cut the apron strings with my parents, so to speak. I had to give her space and time until she was comfortable and ready to say, "You know what, I agree we should move."

So I waited for that moment, which took six months. "Okay, I see it now," she said one day. "Moving is a good decision."

We didn't argue: a win-win.

**Amy:** That's because Michael gave me the time I needed to process that big decision, and when God impressed upon my heart, *I'm going to stretch you* (that we needed to move, to get out on our own), I was on board.

These are the things you'll need to know as you become a couple. If you think your relationship is definitely headed to the altar, you'll definitely want to pay close attention to the next chapter.

## Think About It

## Talk About It

- When preparing to marry and planning your wedding ceremony, why is it wise to invest time and money in quality premarital counseling?

- We advise couples to start practicing LUV Talk (Listening, Understanding, and Validating) early in their relationships. A great way to do this is with drive-through conversation. Why not have some fun with this on a dinner date? Take turns practicing a drive-through discussion, perhaps on an issue that has caused some tension in your relationship. Have fun with this, and have some chocolate mousse for dessert!

- What preparations have you made, either together or separately, for marriage? Keep track of your progress and any personal insights you've made.

# The First **Night Together**

**Michael:** It would be interesting to know the percentage of couples who meet at eHarmony.com (or any of the other proprietary online dating sites) and wind up saying, "I do." Love does "make the world go 'round," and I'm happy for those couples who feel they are more than a match—they were destined to fall in love and marry. If you think your relationship is headed to the altar, this chapter contains our advice for planning a great wedding and honeymoon, although this may be a case of "do as we say and not as we did."

When Amy said yes to my wedding proposal in September 1994, we envisioned a lovely springtime wedding in mid-May of 1995, with bridesmaids richly dressed in champagne satin gowns laced up in the back, and Amy's three-year-old niece, Katie, dropping rose petals on the bride's path.

The month of May, however, was eight months away. Since we were planning to remain celibate, that was too long for us to wait. (Sorry, but that's the blunt truth.) So we moved things up to March. By mid-October, though, Amy and I knew that March wasn't going to work either, so we settled on Saturday, December 17. So what if that date was just two weeks after she and Jeff had planned to get married? From that day forward, it would be *our* wedding anniversary day.

With just two months leading up to our marriage, our prenuptial activity felt as frenetic as the planning in *Father of the Bride,* the hilarious movie starring Steve Martin and Diane Keaton. I had fallen in love with the movie and really liked the wedding march that played while the character of George Banks escorted his daughter, Annie, down the center aisle. I wanted Amy to walk in on her father's arm to the same music, Pachelbel's Canon in D Major, written by German composer and organist Johann Pachelbel in the seventeenth century.

On December 17, precisely at noon at Seventh and James Baptist Church in Waco, Amy looked as radiant as any bride could when David Johnston escorted the youngest of three daughters to the stirring strings of the Pachelbel canon. I might have looked calm while my father and I stood shoulder to shoulder in the sanctuary waiting for them, but I felt a huge pounding in my chest. Nevertheless, I beamed with joy because the day I had dreamed about since I was in third grade—becoming a husband—was happening.

I secretly hoped that Dad wouldn't be so excited that he would forget Amy's name. Our family constantly razzed him about the time he performed the wedding of my best friend from high school, Mario D'Ortenzio, but he couldn't remember the bride's name, which happened to be Karrie.

*We are gathered here today to witness the union of Mario and…and…uh…*
Someone had to whisper Karrie's name to Dad.

But Dad came through with flying colors, and he had the right words
to say as he described marriage as being like a love account. "You will make
withdrawals from and deposits into that love account, but you want your
deposits to outnumber your withdrawals by five to one," I remember him
saying. After Dad pronounced us husband and wife, we hung around the
church for pictures before hopping in a white limo for the short drive to
the reception at the Brazos Club, located on the top floor of the Bank One
building in Waco. Three hundred guests had been invited for a reception
and sit-down buffet. (In case you're wondering, Kathie Lee Gifford couldn't
sing at our reception after all because we had given her such short notice
after moving up the wedding date.)

Weddings are very expensive these days, especially ones with lavish
receptions. What we tell young couples in counseling is that your family
shouldn't feel the pressure to spend twenty-two thousand dollars on a wedding, which is the national average these days, according to Condé Nast
Bridal Infobank.[1] A cake-and-coffee reception in the church fellowship hall
can work just fine. The Johnston and the Smalley parents (my parents
offered to help out) spent some coin because they had the financial resources
to do so. If that's not the case with your family, don't worry about it.

What's really sad about the whole process is that of the twenty-two
thousand dollars young couples spend on their weddings, virtually none
of that goes toward their lives together, like buying a book such as this one
or taking a premarital inventory like PREPARE/ENRICH. Dr. David
Olson, probably the best premarital researcher in the world, did a study
and found that the PREPARE program can predict a couple's divorce rate

with an 80 percent rate of success.² Imagine, if couples took their lives together as seriously as their wedding planning, divorce in this country could drop drastically!

Following the reception, for most couples, is the start of the honeymoon, a time-honored social rite of passage in which a couple shares a bed and their lives for the first time (at least in theory). The honeymoon allows the couple to live together without the pressures of everyday life.

The importance of easing into a new living arrangement has been recognized for a long time. Moses told the Hebrew nation that "a newly married man must not be drafted into the army or given any other responsibilities. He must be free to be at home for one year, bringing happiness to the wife he has married" (Deuteronomy 24:5).

That sounds great to me, having a whole year to hang out with my new wife, but that's just not possible in today's society. Nonetheless, honeymoons retain their allure, especially for couples that haven't cohabited prior to marriage. These days, we are often asked about the honeymoon in our premarital counseling: "Where should we go?" "How long should we go for?"

We have some real simple advice: Pack your swimsuits and suntan oil and drive or fly to a beach resort for a rollicking yet relaxing time. One to two weeks is enough; any longer and it's hard to return to Port Reality. Don't try to fly halfway around the world. This is not the time to reenact a Griswold-like *European Vacation* or go on a hiking trek through Nepalese hinterlands, where privacy and sanitation are scarce. Instead, check into a nice hotel in Hawaii, the Caribbean, Florida, or California. A quiet lakeshore cabin in the mountains will certainly do if that's more your style or you need to trim expenses. Honeymoons are stressful enough, so make life easy on yourself and your young marriage, knowing that there will be adjustments to be made when you're living with someone of the opposite sex.

Did we mention the word *sex*?

If you are not already having sex with each other, then you will have to make sure and learn all you can about sex before your first night together. But don't assume that you know what you're doing just because you've been sexually active before or during this relationship. Many young couples, especially Christian young people, might have had sex, but they feel so guilty about it that they never discuss it—or read books on how to do it better. A honeymoon can turn into a disaster if a couple doesn't know some simple rules about healthy sex and what it takes to please each other sexually. If you're a virgin, as I was, then you probably think sex will be a natural and easy thing to accomplish. But as I learned on my first night, I needed guidance and affirmation!

## SOME DOS AND DON'TS

**Amy:** Michael and I can laugh about it now, but the physical part did take a little practice. Anyway, let's not go there. If you want to see a young couple blush during premarital counseling, ask them what they think the wedding night will be like. Based on *our* experience and talking with others, we usually impart this advice:

- Don't try to fly to your honeymoon destination on the same day as your wedding. Many couples go straight to the airport from the reception, fly half the night to some exotic locale, and arrive at the hotel half-dead following an exhausting but exhilarating twenty-four hours. Even if she's dead to the world, he's still raring to go, so the newly minted husband usually just goes for it. She comes away from her first sexual experience thinking, *That hurts!* That's not making love; that's making sex.

If you are traveling a considerable distance, we recommend staying at an airport hotel and flying out the next morning or afternoon. The whole idea is to have plenty of time to make the first sexual experience good for both of you.

- Get clean. If you think that you can carry her across the threshold, lay her gently on the bed, strip off your sweaty tuxedo, and climb on top of her and go for it, forget it. You smell bad because you've had a nervous sweat going all day. Take a shower, or better yet, suds up with her in one of those oversized bathtubs found in many honeymoon suites. Bathing together is a wonderful way to relax and get clean, and you can definitely have more fun together in a bathtub or shower than when you're alone! Another thing: make sure those fingernails are trimmed, because you're going to be using those fingers in several ways.

- Begin with a massage. I'm not going to tell you that she'll be putty in your hands after you give her a full-body massage, but I will tell you that she will be relaxed. I'm such a great fan of giving massages that I thought at one time about becoming a masseuse.

When Michael would ask me, "Would you like a massage?" I thought he just wanted to give me a relaxing massage—*what a sweetheart.* Him? He was thinking foreplay all the way. He would start giving me a massage, but within five minutes I could tell he was heading in a different direction. One time I said, "I would like to know that when you offer me a massage, you're just going to give me a massage. Now I feel when you ask me if I want a massage, you're really asking me if I want sex."

That prompted Michael to change his spiel. He began asking me, "Would you like an athletic massage or a sexual massage?"

I always cracked up when I heard that. Sometimes I said, "Athletic—I'm sore," and he knew better than to get worked up while he rubbed me. Other times I was bolder, saying coyly, "I think I'll have a sexual massage." That's when he would light the candles, put some soft music on the CD player, and let the magic fingers do their work.

- Keep a towel handy. If on your honeymoon this is her first time having sex, it would be a good idea to put a towel underneath her for the first night or two since she may start to bleed. That may seem kind of goofy, laying down a towel and getting all prepared, but it's practical; making love can get messy.

- Ladies, know that it could be hard to mentally switch gears. You may find it difficult to let go and enjoy your first sexual experience. You may have grown up in a home where it was drilled into you that sex was a sin; maybe you've had a negative sexual encounter; maybe you're just nervous on your wedding night. Although it can be a struggle to overcome those feelings, once you're married, making love is something you can and should enjoy because God gave married couples the gift of sex.

- Take it easy. Cue up the old Eagles song because that needs to be your theme song if you are experiencing each other for the first time. The guy cannot thrust away with reckless abandon. If he does, she will become very sore, especially if she is a virgin. The first couple of nights will not be that fun for her if you're not careful. Don't think you're going to rock'n'roll and go crazy for a few hours, or you may find yourself locked out of the room. It takes a few days or a few weeks for the vagina to become used to the friction involved in lovemaking. Speaking of friction, there's a way to ease the uncomfortable rub: K-Y Jelly. Guys, use it!

Guys who rush end up regretting their actions. Michael had a friend who visited him a few months after his wedding. When asked how things went, Michael's friend broke down and wept. "I had no idea what I was doing," he said. "My honeymoon was a disaster."

"What happened?" my husband probed. The way his friend described it, he went after it way too quick, which made lovemaking very painful for his bride. Of course, she didn't even come close to an orgasm during their honeymoon, and three months later, she still hadn't gone into orbit.

"I don't know what I'm doing," Michael's friend said. "I can't slow down, and I can't calm down. I just go so quick." That's why we always tell guys to take it easy, slow down, don't be in a rush.

- Be flexible on your wedding night. You never know what will happen. This reminds us of a story we heard about a newlywed husband who responded in an incredible way on his wedding night.

When Rick and Lisa were engaged, several friends took Rick aside. "You should know that not all sexual encounters will be a ten, with romantic music playing in the background," one friend said, as Rick nodded his understanding.

Rick and Lisa, in their midtwenties, had been saving themselves for each other. As virgins, they did not want to be unprepared for the start of their sexual relationship, so they read Kevin Leman's *Sex Begins in the Kitchen* and the more graphic *The Gift of Sex* by Cliff and Joyce Penner. (Now *that* took willpower... talking about sex and intimacy but not doing anything about it.)

"One of the last chapters in Leman's book is 'Ying, Yang,' which lists all the slang terms for the penis," said Lisa. "We just cracked up reading that stuff. But what it did was get us verbal about what so many people are afraid to mention: body parts."

Nonetheless, at their last premarital counseling session, their pastor imparted this advice: "Don't expect fireworks on your honeymoon night."

As you can imagine, the young couple was still pretty excited. After the wedding, the long reception, and the drive to their honeymoon getaway, the big moment had arrived. Lisa unpacked two nightgowns and held them up. "Which one should I wear?" she asked her new husband.

When Rick pointed to the pink lace chiffon, Lisa tiptoed into the bathroom. A few moments later, she came out into the darkened room, slipped under the covers, and suddenly realized all the boundaries were gone. All the waiting was over...and she felt sick to her stomach.

Lisa's nerves shot to the ceiling. "Honey, I think I'm going to throw up," she said, as she covered her mouth and bolted to the bathroom.

Rick could hear her heaving away, and when she returned

five minutes later, she was as white as their bed sheets. Lisa lay back and moaned. Rick drew near to her and put his arms around her. "Sweetie, we can just go to sleep. We don't have to have sex tonight."

Can you believe that guy? He deserves some type of reward, and he received it the next morning—and throughout their marriage.

"Let me tell you what it did for me," said Lisa. "What Rick did instilled confidence that he loved me. Here we were, legally married, and we could have sex together, and he said he could wait until I felt better. When I awoke the next morning, I felt complete security over how much he cared for *me* and not my body. Believe me, I woke up raring to go. Rick was a bit surprised, though pleasantly. Afterward, we took a bath together, and I had thought it would be a long time before I could do something like *that* with him. I really believe his sensitivity and gentleness on our wedding night had a lot to do with instilling a great sexual confidence in me."

- Ladies, don't forget to urinate before and afterward. Lovemaking with a full bladder is uncomfortable, so be sure to urinate before. Urinary infections are common for ladies during the honeymoon, which can wipe out having any more lovemaking. So make sure you visit the bathroom soon after having sex—and not just the first time. This advice is so different from what you see in movies. In the world of Hollywood, a couple has sex, and after they're done, they cuddle with each other and fall asleep. Many virgin couples think this is what they should do, but sex is a messy thing, and you don't want a lack of knowledge to ruin your time together.

- Do some homework. Did you notice that Rick and Lisa said they read a couple of sex-ed books prior to their wedding night? While you have to be careful that you're not pouring kerosene on a small fire, we recommend reading up on sex before actually experiencing it. Michael had watched the videos based on the best-selling book, *Intended for Pleasure: Sex Technique & Sexual Fulfillment in Christian Marriage,* by Ed Wheat, MD, and his wife, Gaye, (now there's a title that tells you exactly what the book is about). He learned some things that he didn't learn in Human Sexuality 101—like what the clitoris was; he wouldn't have had any idea about what it would take to make his wife really excited.

  You should consult the Wheats' book (or *Sheet Music: Uncovering the Secrets of Sexual Intimacy in Marriage* by Kevin Leman) for details, but making love starts with foreplay, and it's foreplay that makes or breaks a woman's enjoyment of sex. A husband who takes his time (there's that reminder again!) and builds up his wife's arousal slowly but surely will find her a much more willing partner.

  **Michael:** Before I got married, I thought couples peaked simultaneously, just as they did in the movies. Wrong! When that did not happen for us, I began stressing. *Man,* I thought, *I must not be doing too good.*

  I didn't know that it can be difficult for a woman to reach a climax during vaginal intercourse. A woman needs stimulating motions around the clitoris with the fingers, and her sexual response is likely to result in a climax when her arousal is allowed to build. As you begin your sexual lives together, you should incorporate clitoral stimulation into your foreplay so that she is not cheated out of orgasmic fulfillment. The French, who have a reputation as sophisticated lovers, have an old saying: "There is no such thing as frigid women, only inept men."

In a sense, I'm there to serve Amy, and she's there to serve me. I'm excited to bring her to orgasm first. She is excited about letting me wait because she knows that's best for me. Biologically, once a man has reached climax, he'd rather eat mud than have sex. The urgent feeling is gone. That's why he has to look after her needs first. If the husband is satisfied in thirty seconds, rolls over, and says, "Thanks, honey," that's not going to do it. Sex always has to be about the other person.

• Talk about what you like. Very few couples ever talk about what's pleasurable to them, which is sad. Amy and I are lucky because we find it easy to talk about sex. We've both studied and experienced clinical psychology, and you become desensitized somewhat because you're talking about penises and vaginas a great deal.

We know a couple who told us that the husband said, "Gosh, I would like something other than the missionary position. How about a little creativity?" His wife told him to forget it. No oral sex, no serious foreplay, and nothing other than the missionary style. Oh, and it'd better be darker than a cemetery at midnight. He was struggling with that. When he asked her whether she could be on top sometimes, she wouldn't even discuss it. What's even more sad is that she wouldn't even talk about where her sexual fears had come from.

Here's where the servant mentality comes in. If it bothers her emotionally to do anything other than the missionary thing, then she should get help and figure out why. Within a context of a healthy sexual relationship, she needs counseling if making love in a different position is too much for her. Maybe her mother scared her and said she would go to hell if she assumed anything other than the missionary position. Searching out the roots of the fears and dealing with them is essential for a healthy sex life.

Let's discuss oral sex again, which is a topic commonly raised in our counseling practice. Let's say the husband wants oral sex, but his wife is grossed out by the thought of having his penis in her mouth. It literally makes her gag. The worst thing the husband can say is, "You're such a prude. Why can't you pleasure me the way I want to be pleasured?" Nagging, demeaning, or pressuring her for oral sex is a sure way of never making it happen.

Be aware that a wife's personality usually doesn't change as she moves from the living room to the bedroom. In other words, a more conservative wife will most likely be more traditional in bed. Our advice: let it go, because that is another way you can serve her. Maybe you can revisit the topic later when it can be emotionally safer to discuss.

Safety always creates boldness. Ladies, if you don't want to have oral sex at first, you might need to at least give it a try with an honest attempt. Your preconceived ideas about oral sex might be wrong.

- Sexual frequency will drop. Sexual frequency, which skyrockets during the honeymoon, drops like Enron stock not long after the honeymoon. We went from three times a day (a morning eye-opener, an afternoon delight, and a nightcap) during the honeymoon to four times a week when we set up housekeeping together. Within a few months, frequency dwindled to the usual once a week. But that was fine with me. These days, I'm like a camel: a good sexual experience can tide me over for a while.

- Remember that the big goal is not orgasms. Oneness is what you're after. True sexual fulfillment comes through a oneness where the two become one and selflessly give to each other. If your goal in sex is orgasm, then you're going to lose.

   One time, Amy and I were discussing sexual intimacy, and I said the sexual relationship is often a barometer of how well the marriage is going: a couple rarely has a great love life when their relationship is marked by disagreements and dysfunction.

   "I don't think that's true," said Amy.

   "Why?" I asked. We like to debate these things.

   "I have a client right now who is married and is in a horrible relationship, but she says her sex is great. So what do you think of your little theory now?"

   "Well, let me tell you," I said. "I would say that she doesn't know how good sex could be."

   She might be having orgasms, but she's not having great sex. Hers isn't great because greatness comes out of a great relationship and oneness. Emotional connectedness makes for the best sex.

- Enjoy the anticipation, because there isn't anything better. An old joke says that when women iron, they think about sex, and when they have sex, they think about ironing. If only men understood what gets women in the mood for love!

Well, I have another story for you, and it's about anticipation, which is a great skill to have when it comes to sex. Anticipation helps get the engines started for our wives. My father used to say that when it came to sex, men are like microwave ovens and women are like Crockpots.

Anyway, on this particular occasion, I woke up around 6:00 a.m. feeling frisky, which is normal for men because our testosterone levels get refueled during the night. Knowing it wasn't fair to throw myself at Amy for a morning quickie (which wives can do from time to time for fun), I rolled over and asked her if she would want to have sex that evening after her counseling sessions. At that time, Amy was counseling on Tuesday nights, which meant that I needed to get home around 4:00 p.m. and take over house duties with the kids.

"Maybe," she replied, which was all I needed to start the anticipation ball rolling.

Throughout the day, we talked on the phone, and I can assure you that sex became more and more prominent on Amy's mind. Guys have some intuition about this matter. I figured that we were going to have some fun that evening after she returned home.

After Amy left for her counseling appointments, I knew there was a long list of things I needed to accomplish before she got home. I had to feed the kids, get them bathed and ready for bed, and then clean up the house, at least the downstairs, because ain't nothin' was going to happen if Amy came home to a messy house. And let me remind you, I was ready for something to happen!

I fed the kids right away and hustled them off to baths, and I must have been so excited about the evening plans that I started putting the kids down for bed at 5:30 p.m. I'll never forget my oldest son looking up to me as I tucked him under the covers: "But Daddy, it's still bright outside. Why am I going to sleep so early?"

I replied with all the gravity of Ward Cleaver. "You'll understand one day, Son."

After getting the kids to bed, I raced downstairs to clean up. The living room was a mess! I'd had too much fun wrestling with the kids, and now I needed to get serious about picking up their toys and straightening things up. So I put stuff away, tucked some things under the couch, and entered the kitchen, which was going to be Amy's first point of entry back into the house. I knew that in her eyes, the kitchen was the most important area of the house and had to be spick-and-span.

I had something working in my favor: the knowledge that that there was a particular smell that, well, let's just say did the trick for Amy in terms of turning her on sexually. I'm not talking about a cologne or some kind of potpourri, but the soothing fragrance of Formula 409—yes, the degreaser found under millions of kitchen sinks. That smell gets Amy's engines revving better than the most ancient aphrodisiac.

I grabbed that bottle of Formula 409 and started spraying it everywhere. On the countertops, on the hardwood floor, on kitchen cabinets, under my arms; the scent of ammonia was so strong that I thought I'd spent an entire evening in Mr. Clean's apartment.

I got everything tidied up, rinsed dishes and stacked them in the dishwasher, and I even remembered to turn the dishwasher on. At that point I began to understand why women aren't usually in the mood after a long day of taking care of the kids and cleaning the house, but I was a man, a tough guy who could fight through fatigue just fine!

I lit some candles, plunked down in my favorite chair, and turned on SportsCenter while I waited for Amy to return home. A half hour later, I heard the garage door go up, so I quickly turned off the television and froze. I was nervous, thinking that I might have forgotten to clean something, which would ruin the night. Amy opened the door from the garage, and I heard each footstep as she walked into the kitchen.

Then, everything stopped. I could hardly breathe because the tension was so high. From the living room, I heard no more footsteps in the kitchen and not a peep from Amy. Right then, I figured I must have left something out, which would zap all my well-laid plans.

Then suddenly I heard a sultry voice from behind me, a voice that carried a very sexy tone as she asked, "Is that the dishwasher?"

Judging by her tone of voice, I thought she was going to say something like, "Is that my hunk of burning love?" But that's not what she said.

So I got up from my chair with the intention of matching her in this game she was playing with me.

"Why…yes, it is the dishwasher," I said back in an equally sexy tone.

She batted her eyes. "You have no idea how that sound turns me on," she replied salaciously.

*Whoa!*

"Well," I said, "just so you know, it's on the *hot* cycle."

Let me tell you, after that, she was putty in my arms, and the day of anticipation turned into an awesome night of experience!

## LOVE STORY

As you can tell, I love my wife, and although our marriage has had it ups and downs like any marital union, it's been a great journey. The following is the final personal story we want to share in this book, because it turned out to be an event that proved my love to Amy. We are sharing this story because we're confident that many young couples often arrive at such a yellow-brick-road moment early in their young and maturing marriages. The decision of which path you take is often *huge* for a young marriage.

Three years after the honeymoon, Amy was a young mom with an infant son, but she had not abandoned her dream of earning a graduate degree in family counseling. Meanwhile, I was rolling along and well into my second and final year of graduate school at Wheaton College, where Amy was in her first year of postgraduate studies in marriage and family counseling.

The pressure of sharing child-raising duties of Cole while both of us attended school was almost overwhelming. Some of our fights, I'm sad to say, were doozies, but my outbursts stemmed from the pressure I was feeling to graduate and get working. After more than six years of college and post-graduate studies, I was tired of school. I wanted to be a man and make a living.

I arrived home from my internship late one night around ten, and when I stepped into our modest townhouse, I looked at Amy and knew something had happened. "Wait a minute," I said. "You're pregnant, aren't you?"

I don't know why I asked, because we were practicing birth control and trying *not* to get pregnant, but something in the look on her face told me that I was right.

Amy began weeping inconsolably. "I-I took the pregnancy test this morning," she blurted.

"And you're pregnant?"

She nodded her weeping face several times.

I threw my arms around her. "I'm so sorry," I said, and I meant it. We were just getting back on our feet after Cole's birth, and Amy had been able to return to school. Since she had another eighteen months to go before graduation, baby number two definitely did not fit into our plans. "What are we going to do?"

As soon as I asked the question, I knew the answer. We would finish out the school year at Wheaton; that way I could graduate in May and not interrupt my studies and internship. Then we would move back to Branson (where we were planning to live once our schooling days were done) so that we could be closer to family and friends who could help out with the children. Meanwhile, I would start my counseling practice and begin working with my father and brother, Greg, at the Smalley Relationship Center.

When Amy was ready, she could finish her graduate program at Evangel University in nearby Springfield, about an hour north of Branson. It wouldn't be the ideal setup, but under the circumstances, it was the wisest and most prudent approach to solving a sticky problem.

Amy, to my painful surprise, was thinking along different lines. She painted the following scenario: We would continue to live in Wheaton after I graduated in the late spring. Following the birth of our second child that summer, I would become Mr. Mom while Amy returned to school in the fall to finish her second and final year at Wheaton College, a place of refuge, great friends, and incredible teaching. In other words, no worky for Mikey, at least outside the home.

Initially, after sharing our positions, we politely clashed. When we saw that neither of us was budging an inch, we turned up the heat with explosive outbursts. That went on for about three weeks, and, during interludes, we did our best to avoid each other, but the issue was never very far from our minds. One afternoon, I was helping Amy with the laundry in the basement when we got into a Tyson-Lennox tussle. She screamed at me and then ran upstairs.

"Don't you run!" I yelled back. It was time to have this out, once and for all. I sprinted after her, but I was too late: she slammed the door in my face and clicked the deadbolt.

"Open up!" I pounded. "Open up!"

I was locked in the basement until Amy consented to let me rejoin the land of the living. Now I was furious, and we ripped each other with invective as only two people familiar with therapy could. I said that I was sick of her selfish attitude, that she was trying to rule me, and anyone as stupid as she was could see that we had to move back to Branson so that we could get some help from my family.

To my surprise, my arguments failed to dislodge her from her position. She insisted that we stay in Wheaton so she could go to school and finish what she had started while I stayed home with the two children.

"But we're talking about an infant!" I pointed out.

"You can bring the little one to me at school, and I'll breast-feed there," she said.

"That is about the stupidest idea I've heard yet!"

I looked at my watch. It was time for me to leave because I had a counseling appointment. In the irony of ironies, I was supposed to help a young couple with *their* marriage…because they were in conflict. What a joke.

I was in no emotional shape to counsel others when I arrived at my off-campus internship office. Since I had a few extra moments, I sought out my supervisor in her office. Without looking up from her desk, she said, "I think we need a time of prayer and silence."

I guess God must have prepared her heart, because what happened next was definitely a God thing. I was at an impasse. I could not see where Amy and I could possibly find a win-win solution to our conflict. Either we stay and I lose, or we move and she loses.

Within a few minutes, I found myself lying on a couch, weeping my heart out and feeling miserable. Suddenly, in my darkness, I saw in my mind an arm come and purposely lay itself down on a wooden plank. It was so vivid that I opened my eyes to figure out what had just happened. God reassured me, and I closed my eyes again. Then I saw a second arm come out of the darkness and lay itself willingly on the wooden cross. I watched as these gigantic, nine-inch nails came out of the darkness and plunged into the wrists of Christ's arms. That's when God spoke to me and said, *Trust me, I know what I'm doing. Do you know what you're doing? What is your problem with serving your wife as I have served the church? Are you telling Me that you can't stay at home for a school year for your wife? Your job is very, very simple as a husband: it's to serve your wife and your children.*

"I've got it! Problem solved!" I exclaimed. My supervisor looked at me as though I had risen from the dead. "Listen," I explained. "I have found a win-win solution, which is for me to stay home. It's a win for me because I get to serve Amy like I'm supposed to. It's a win for her because she gets to pursue her dream—a counseling degree."

I had the greatest counseling session with the young married couple. Then I rushed home because I had left Amy in a precarious state.

"Amy, problem solved," I said as I soon as I stepped in the front door.

Of course, she was still thinking about how much of a jerk I had been. "Who are you to come to me and say that's it's solved? This is nowhere near being solved."

"Wait, wait, please let me explain. Look, God showed me tonight that my job is to serve you."

"Really?"

"Yes, really. I just want you to know that if it's important for you to stay here and finish school, if you need me to be a stay-at-home dad, then that is what I'm going to do, and I'm excited to do it."

The three weeks of anger and frustration in her face melted instantly. Amy threw her arms around me, and it was awesome. We were both so relieved that we began to experience the full oneness that God intended.

## A NEW LIFE

I kept my word. Following graduation, we continued to live in Wheaton as Amy's pregnancy progressed. In June, our daughter Reagan was born, and two months later, Amy returned to graduate school while I stayed with the kids during the day.

You should have seen me. I was Michael Keaton of *Mr. Mom*, the stay-at-home-dad who fed and played and napped with a toddler son and an infant daughter all day long. Of course, who wants to be cooped up in a townhouse all day? I liked fresh air just as much as any adult, so each day at noontime, I bundled up Cole and Reagan, put them in their car seats, and drove them to the Yorktown Mall for a stroll and something to eat. I wasn't the only one to come up with this idea: after a while, I met a half-dozen stay-at-home moms with their children at the food court. As we stuffed crackers into the mouths of our young ones, we would talk about mom stuff—like Wal-Mart's falling prices on Gerber's baby food and Marshalls' great sale on OshKosh clothing.

Cole and Reagan, I noticed at the food court, eventually wore whatever I fed them. Necessity being the father of invention, I stripped the children down to their diapers before letting them eat and drink away. The other moms were shocked at my behavior, but from what I saw, skin cleaned up much faster than clothing—and didn't stain.

After a few weeks I started noticing that other babies in the food court were also naked like my children. In fact, a group of moms approached me and let me know what a brilliant parent I was.

I looked at them and said, "No more stains, huh?"

A lot of heads nodded in agreement. "No more stains," they said.

God gave me the grace to accept my new position as Mr. Mom with a great heart. I was rewarded in unexpected ways. For instance, I played more golf that year than any other year in my entire life. Every weekend—or whenever Amy had an afternoon off from school—she pushed me out the door and told me to go play eighteen holes. What I started learning is that from the moment I gave up all my expectations, I got everything I had previously hoped for.

Our relationship marched toward oneness. That year was probably the single most defining time in our marriage, because it clued us in to the true meaning of love and serving each other. Sure, we weren't perfect, but when I began serving Amy, she looked for ways she could serve me.

I think it's safe to say that I never would have been a stay-at-home dad if I hadn't done it that year for Amy. That decision carried an unintended consequence, which is this: since 95–98 percent of husbands never get a chance to be a stay-at-home parent, they listen when I talk about that experience at my speaking engagements.

God knew what He was doing, because as a result, I've been able to share this story with tens of thousands of men over the last five years. I give them the message that *hey, you can do this—you can serve your wife.* I tell them that I don't mean they *have* to quit their jobs and be stay-at-home dads for a period, but there are certainly other avenues of service available in a marriage.

One weekend I was speaking at a Promise Keepers conference, and during the Saturday evening session, I stepped out on the platform dressed in a white toga and wearing an oversized, glow-in-the-dark hoop earring. I challenged the men that night to become bond servants to their families.

A bond servant, I explained, was someone who had been given his freedom from his master but who chose to stay with his master as his servant. When that happened, the bond servant became a slave to his master for the rest of his life (and typically he was not mistreated).

To seal the deal between the two parties ("I'll be your lifelong servant, and you'll treat me well"), the master would take his new bond servant to the home's doorpost and pierce his earlobe with a large hoop earring to signify their special relationship.

Not long after I delivered that message, I received a letter from a pastor who said, "I just want you to know that I heard your sermon at the Promise Keepers event in Atlanta. I'm a forty-four-year-old Southern Baptist, balding, overweight pastor who just went to Wal-Mart to get his ear pierced with a hoop earring so I will never forget what my position should be in the family. I have to write you to let you know how much what you said impacted my life. For the first time in my life, I realized what my job is."

You may be wondering if I wear a hoop earring, if I put my money where my mouth is. The answer is no, but if this book sells a hundred thousand copies, I'll get my left ear pierced and wear a gold hoop earring on occasion. That's a promise that I hope I get to keep.

**Amy:** As we close our time together, do you feel you know us? You'd better, because Michael and I shared from our hearts and opened up old wounds for an important reason: to help you have the best relationship humanly possible. I would imagine that if you've found a special person, well-meaning friends may have offered this advice: "Just wait. Everything will change after you get married."

Are they right? Our answer is, well…yes and no. Before Michael and I married, we thought we knew a lot about each other. I knew that I certainly liked what I saw, so much so that I envisioned a happily-ever-after scenario for myself. I really bought into the idea that if I was marrying the son of America's marriage expert, life would be a bed of rose petals, right?

Wrong! The first year was as wobbly as a circus performer who's learning to walk a tightrope. Our relationship didn't get on solid ground until we straightened out a few things and learned how to resolve conflict, as we've described in this book.

But as I look back to what got us through those rocky times, I know why our relationship survived: commitment. We made a solemn promise before God, before our families, and before our friends that we were in this marriage for the long haul. Even with that promise, I still struggled the first year, wondering what I had gotten myself into. It was only the commitment I had made to God, myself, and my husband that weathered us through. Let me assure you, it has been so worth it.

No matter where you are in life—in a relationship, looking for a relationship, or wondering if there will ever *be* a relationship—we want you to remember that there will come a time when you'll have to cast all doubts to the wind and follow the commitment you made in your heart. Romans 12:1–2 says, "I urge you, brothers, in view of God's mercy, to offer your bodies as living sacrifices, holy and pleasing to God—this is your spiritual act of worship. Do not conform any longer to the pattern of this world, but be transformed by the renewing of your mind" (NIV).

I did this daily for many months. When you want to bail, transform your mind. Don't let yourself go there! Scott Stanley, in his book *The Heart of Commitment,* wrote about making a meta-commitment, which is the commitment to being committed.

You know, there were times when I blew up at Michael, but I'll never forget one occasion when his quiet words spoke his commitment to me.

"Amy, I'm not going anywhere," he said with palms outstretched. "I'm staying right here. No matter how much you fight me, I'm going to love you forever."

Wow! That affirming statement, which he backed up with action, stabilized me enough to the point where I wanted to change, I wanted to love him, and I wanted to be with him forever.

Writing about those experiences gives me such pleasure and prompts me to remind you that if you want to stay committed, nurture your relationship. Guard your words. Avoid certain places and people. Recognize that an affair can happen to you.

If you are not married yet, do one more thing before you say "I do." As objectively as you can, write down on a two-column sheet of paper all the compatible and incompatible areas you have with your potential spouse. Write out all the strengths and weaknesses. Now ask yourself these questions:

- Are you compatible in the areas of life most important to you?
- Can you live with his or her weaknesses for the rest of your life?
- Are you ready to be committed in marriage for the rest of your life?

When you're ready to make that commitment, and your special person is ready as well, then both of you are prepared to say, "I do."

There's a saying that sums up marriage quite nicely: "Love isn't an act; it's a whole life." As your relationship moves forward, you'll walk onto the stage of many new acts, and the play doesn't end until the Lord draws the curtain.

## Think About It

## Talk About It

- What are your expectations for your honeymoon? Are there any expectations that might need reevaluation so that you don't experience a honeymoon disaster like ours?
- What do you really want from the physical side of your marriage? Do your expectations match the mutual servanthood model of helping each other experience sexual satisfaction?
- What are some ways to focus on the romance of that part of your life together?

# Notes

## Chapter 1

1. Mary Madden and Amanda Lenhart, *Online Dating* (Washington DC: Pew Internet & American Life Project, March 5, 2006), ii.
2. Madden and Lenhart, *Online Dating,* i.
3. Ellen Gamerman, "Mismatched.com," *Wall Street Journal,* April 1, 2006, 1.
4. "Beware of Online Dating Fakers," ABC News, February 12, 2006, www.abcnews.com/GMA/story?id=1608836&page=1.
5. Dr. David Olson, quoted in Helena Oliviero, "More Couples Get Premarital Counseling," *Atlanta Journal and Constitution,* May 28, 2002, http://lists101.his.com/pipermail/smartmarriages/2002-May/001149.html.

## Chapter 2

1. U.S. Census Bureau, "Living Together, Living Alone: Families and Living Arrangements, 2000," Part II, Chapter 5, Population Profile of the United States: 2000, 5-1, www.census.gov/population/pop-profile/2000/chap05.pdf.
2. David Popenoe and Barbara Dafoe Whitehead, "Should We Live

Together? What Young Adults Need to Know About Cohabitation Before Marriage," The National Marriage Project, January 1999, 3, quoted in *The Family Portrait: A Compilation of Data, Research and Public Opinion on the Family,* Family Research Council, Washington DC, 2002, 82.

3. Centers for Disease Control and Prevention, "Trends in Reportable Sexually Transmitted Diseases in the United States, 2004: National Surveillance Data for Chlamydia, Gonorrhea, and Syphillis," November 2005, 1, www.cdc.gov/std/stats/04pdf/trends2004.pdf.

4. Bureau of Justice Statistics, *Highlights from 20 Years of Surveying Crime Victims: The National Crime Victimization Survey, 1973-92,* U.S. Department of Justice, Washington, DC, September 1993, 25, as quoted in *The Family Portrait,* published by the Family Research Council, 2002.

5. Bureau of Justice Statistics, *Highlights from 20 Years of Surveying Crime Victims,* as quoted in *The Family Portrait,* published by the Family Research Council, 2002.

6. Barbara Dafoe Whitehead and David Popenoe, "The State of Our Unions: The Social Health of Marriage in America 2002," The National Marriage Project, Rutgers, Piscataway, NJ, June 2002, 6, http://marriage.rutgers.edu.

7. Chuck Colson, "For Better or Worse...Mostly Worse," *Southern California Christian Times,* September 2002, 8.

8. Pamela Paul, "About the Book," www.startermarriage.com.

9. Pamela Paul interview, "'Starter Marriages': Are Gen Xers Really Ready to Walk down the Aisle?" *Good Morning America,* January 25, 2002.

## Chapter 4

1. These statements are paraphrased from the PREPARE Couple Inventory and are used with permission of Dr. David Olson and Life Innovations.

2. James Houran, PhD, "The Truth About Compatibility Testing," *Online Dating Magazine,* www.onlinedatingmagazine.com/features/ compatibilitytesting.html.

3. These categories are taken from the PREPARE Couple Iventory and are used with permission from Dr. David Olson and Life Innovations.

## Chapter 5

1. This story, which has been slightly changed by the authors, circulates widely on the Internet.

2. National Center for Health Statistics, *Health, United States, 2005,* Hyattsville, Maryland, 2005, 64.

3. The Personality Profile for Couples CD, which contains the personality test, is available on the Web at www.dnaofrelationships.com.

4. Material in bold quoted from David Swift, Enneagram Research, Development & Applications, www.enneagraminstitute.com.

5. Renee Baron and Elizabeth Wagele, *The Enneagram Made Easy: Discover the Nine Types of People* (San Francisco: HarperCollins, 1994).

## Chapter 6

1. "Desperate for a call, and other hang-ups," November 27, 2004, www.theage.com.au.

## Chapter 7

1. Les and Leslie Parrott, *Relationships* (Grand Rapids, MI: Zondervan, 1998), 138.

2. Chip Ingram, *Love, Sex & Lasting Relationships* (Grand Rapids, MI: Baker, 2003), 188.

3. Anonymous, "Romances with Wolves," Campus Crusade for Christ, 1997, www.everystudent.com/features/wolves.html.

## Chapter 8

1. Scott Stanley, Daniel Trathen, Savanna McCain, and Milt Bryan, *A Lasting Promise: A Christian Guide to Fighting for Your Marriage* (New York: Jossey-Bass, 1998).

2. Gary Smalley, *Secrets to Lasting Love: Uncovering the Keys to Lifelong Intimacy* (New York: Fireside, 2000).

3. "Eight Unusual Ways to Create Cash," May 2, 2005, www.freemoney finance.com/2005/05/eight_unusual_w.html.

4. "Top Things to Know," Money 101, Lesson 9, http://money.cnn.com/ pf/101/lessons/9/.

5. Robert Ebbin, "Americans' Dining-Out Habits," *Restaurants USA*, November 2000, www.restaurant.org/rusa/magArticle.cfm?Article ID=138.

## Chapter 9

1. Howard J. Markman, Scott M. Stanley, and Susan L. Blumberg, *Fighting for Your Marriage: Positive Steps for Preventing Divorce and Preserving a Lasting Love* (New York: Jossey-Bass, 2001).

## Chapter 10

1. "Marriott Woos Newlyweds," *Pacific Business News* (Honolulu), 1, April 21, 2004, http://pacific.bizjournals.com/pacific/stories/2004/04/19/daily43.htm.

2. Dr. Olson, quoted in Helena Oliviero, "More Couples Get Premarital Counseling," *Atlanta Journal and Constitution,* May 28, 2002, http://lists101.his.com/pipermail/smartmarriages/2002-May/001149.html.

# Want to Learn More About Michael and Amy or Hear Them Speak?

Visit their Web site at www.amyandmichael.org, where you can read articles and take relationship tests. You can also use the Web site to book Amy and Michael to speak at your special events, Sunday services, or singles and marriage seminars.

## THE SMALLEY MARRIAGE AND FAMILY CENTER
### WWW.SMALLEYMARRIAGECENTER.COM

Thinking of asking that special person to marry you? Does your marriage need a tune-up? Then consider traveling to Michael and Amy's new full-service counseling and training center outside of Houston. The Smalley Marriage and Family Center, located in The Woodlands, Texas, provides two critical services to help singles and married couples experience phenomenal relationships:

1. Premarital training/counseling. The Smalleys' premarital service uses Dr. David Olson's incredibly successful and well-researched program PREPARE/ENRICH. Over two million couples have experienced this high-impact curriculum.

2. Marriage retreats. If your relationship needs a break from the normal stress and conflicts of daily life, then the Smalley marriage retreats will be perfect for you. Whether you're contemplating divorce or seeking a fun trip away from home, the Smalley retreats are designed to increase your satisfaction, eliminate divorce, and rejuvenate your marriage in the pristine setting of The Woodlands, Texas.

Each retreat will teach you valuable skills to ensure a lifetime of happiness, and there are enjoyable diversions as well: shopping at a nearby mall and outdoor shopping plazas, entertainment (concerts, movies, and more), and golf on fabulous courses designed by Arnold Palmer, Jack Nicklaus, Tom Fazio, and Gary Player.

For more information, go to www.smalleymarriagecenter.com or contact the Smalley Marriage and Family Center at 2200 Lake Woodlands Drive, The Woodlands, Texas 77380. Telephone: (281) 466-8602.

# About the Authors

Michael and Amy Smalley hold master's degrees in clinical psychology with an emphasis in marriage and family. For more than eight years, they've shared their trusted experience with young and veteran couples, giving straightforward and no-nonsense advice to thousands around the world.

Michael and Amy have participated in several video series including *Secrets to Lasting Love*, *Solving the Real Love in the Real World Puzzle*, and *The Secret to Sexual Intimacy*, and they are the coauthors of the book *Don't Date Naked*. Michael was also a coauthor of *The DNA of Relationships* with Gary Smalley (which Amy also contributed to) and of *Communicating with Your Teen* with his brother Dr. Greg Smalley.

The Smalleys, who are the parents of three children, Cole, Reagan, and David, make their home just outside of Houston, Texas.

To learn more about WaterBrook Press and view
our catalog of products, log on to our Web site:
**www.waterbrookpress.com**

WATERBROOK
PRESS